THE STANDARD WINE COOK BOOK

The Standard Wine Cook Book

BY ANNE DIRECTOR

Ross Books
P.O. Box 4340
Berkeley, Ca 94704

Library of Congress Cataloging in Publication Data

Director, Anne.
The Standard Wine Cookbook.

Includes index.

1. Cookery (Wine) I. Title.
TX726.D5 1978 641.6'2 77-28047
ISBN 0-89496-013-X

Acknowledgments

My sincere appreciation is herewith extended to the California Wine Advisory Board and the Wine Institute, for their co-operation and permission to use the chart of wine types and many of the excellent recipes which appear in this book. To J.Mc.G. and E.P.H. my heartfelt thanks for their encouragement and assistance.

—ANNE DIRECTOR

Contents

THE STANDARD
WINE COOK BOOK

CHAPTER 1

WINE IN COOKING

In those countries where wines are commonly used with food they also are commonly introduced into food in cooking. They lose their alcohol when subjected to heat, but chefs depend upon them to heighten the flavor and aroma of foods and to give them balance.

ENCYCLOPAEDIA BRITANNICA

I once heard a famous chef describe wine in cooking as the "magic ingredient." When you've discovered for yourself the new zest and flavor that wine lends to foods, I think you'll agree. For wine not only accents all the good natural flavors of foods, but adds a delightful fragrance and flavor which transforms many a humdrum, prosaic dish into a festive offering.

Perhaps you've thought of wine as something mysterious and complicated. If so, you've a pleasant surprise in store for you. There's nothing difficult about cooking with wine once you recognize that it is used just as you use other seasonings; you add wine as easily as you add salt and pepper. The celebrated cooks of France and other countries use wine in cooking as naturally as we use water. In fact, wine is used in place of water, and if you've tasted a deliciously prepared dish and wondered about its elusive flavoring, the answer undoubtedly is wine!

Wine itself is not detectible when used in cooking, for it blends with the food flavors to create something new and richer. It is well to remember this: if you taste wine in your cooking, *you've used too much!* What you want is the delicate, subtle fragrance and flavor which wine imparts, but you don't want it to dominate the dish.

When wine is used in cooking the alcohol evaporates just as it does when vanilla is used. What remains is the delicious flavor of the grapes blended with the flavor of the food.

I'm frequently asked, "What *kind* of wine is used in cooking?" This is a good time to point out that you don't need a special kind of wine for cooking. Simply use some of the table wine you've selected to serve as a beverage with your dinner. Steal a cup or whatever amount you need from the same bottle, and add it to your cooking, or use it to baste when broiling or baking.

Any of the red table wines, such as Claret and Burgundy, or the white table wines, such as Sauterne or Rhine Wine, may be used to advantage. These and other wines are described in the next chapter.

Sherry, one of the world's most famous wines, is a perennial favorite in the kitchen. This distinctive nutty-flavored wine blends with almost every kind of food. Sherry is used extensively in soups and with fish and shellfish. It adds superb flavor to many chicken dishes, to ham and other meats, and is excellent for serving over fresh fruits.

Port, Muscatel, and Tokay are the sweeter wines and are, therefore, natural companions of sweeter foods, such as desserts, fruits, and dessert sauces.

Each wine has its individual flavor and each contributes its characteristic flavor to the food with which it is combined. Try different wines with the same foods. For example, let's say you're preparing lamb stew. In the meat section of this book you'll find a recipe specifying Sauterne or Rhine Wine. After you have enjoyed the lamb stew accented with Sauterne you will probably want to try this same recipe with Rhine Wine for a delicately different flavor. Perhaps you'll want to explore further flavor variations and try the lamb stew combined with still another member of the white table wine family, such as Chablis. Or you might add a completely new and different flavor by substituting a red table wine, such as Claret or Burgundy.

There are no rules you must follow, but in general the red table wines are most successfully employed in dishes made with red meats or other dishes where dark ingredients are used; the white table wines in dishes made with white meats, chicken, and seafood.

There are really only two fundamental points to remember when using wine in cooking. The first, which we mentioned earlier in this chapter and repeat here for added emphasis, is: always use a little *less* wine, rather than a little more, to accent but not to dominate the recipe. The second: heat wine, but *do not boil* it. For example, when flavoring soups, the wine is added just before removing the soup from the stove. In preparing sauces, the wine is usually the last ingredient and is only simmered in the sauce.

Here, then, you will find recipes for foods that will taste new and different and exciting; soups and salads and sauces to which wine adds piquant flavor and dramatic interest; vegetables, eggs, and cheese dishes; meats, poultry, and fish prepared with wine to increase the enjoyment of a meal.

The section devoted to fruits, desserts, and dessert sauces offers a variety of distinctive yet easy-to-prepare desserts, exquisitely wine-flavored to lend a lavish and elegant air to your dinners. Last but not least are the wine beverages—the traditional wine punches and champagne bowls, the coolers, cocktails, and cobblers which have been favorites for generations and which are enjoying renewed popularity in these days of more moderate home entertaining.

To aid you in acquiring ease and familiarity with wine, the following chapter describes the differences between the sweet or dessert wines and the so-called "dry" or table wines. Charts are included to enable you to recognize readily the various wine names and classifications.

The Wine Service Guide identifies appropriate wines for service before dinner, with foods, for dessert or refreshment, and sets forth information on temperatures, table service, and glassware. Pertinent and valuable suggestions on selecting and buying wines, wine storing and care, are offered in Chapter 4.

And now to you who are about to read and use this book a toast to your better eating. May you find, as did Shakespeare, that "Good wine is a good familiar creature, if it be well used." May wine lend inspiration to your cooking, new sparkle and spice to your enjoyment of dining!

CHAPTER 2

HOW TO RECOGNIZE DIFFERENT WINES, WINE NAMES AND CLASSIFICATIONS

Wine that maketh glad the heart of man.

PSALM 104:15 (OLD TESTAMENT)

Vintners speak of wine-*growing*, for wine is truly a product of Nature. It is the pure, naturally fermented juice of fresh ripe grapes and man's role is solely to guide the development, constantly watching to see that Nature does her work to perfection.

The kind of wine depends upon the kind of grapes from which it comes. Most wines are blended from the juice of two or more grape varieties, and such blending is an art requiring great skill and a comprehensive knowledge of grape flavors and characteristics.

RED WINES AND WHITE WINES

When wines are to be red, the grape juice is fermented with the skin of the grapes. The natural pigment of the skin enters the wine, giving these wines their rich red color and a light, pleasantly tart flavor.

For white wines, the juice is separated from the pulp and skins, as the juice from even the darkest-colored grapes is almost always a clear white.

DRY WINES

When wines are described as "dry" it simply means that those wines are not essentially sweet to the taste. The juice of all grapes is sweet before fermentation, and the sweetness of wines is the natural sweetness of the grape juice. When the grapes are pressed the juice naturally ferments. When this natural fermentation process is completed, most of the sweetness disappears. The resultant wines are called "dry."

The dry wines are largely the red table wines, such as Claret and Burgundy, and the white table wines, such as Sauterne and Rhine Wine. These wines are delicately tart and tangy, not sweet. They blend superbly with food flavors and their primary use is with foods and in wine cookery. The alcohol content of these table wines ranges from 10 per cent to 14 per cent by volume.

SWEET WINES

No sweetening is added to wines. When a sweeter wine is desired, the natural fermentation process is halted by the addition of a little pure grape brandy. This brandy is distilled from wine and is the pure essence of the grape. Strict state and federal laws and regulations prohibit the addition of any other kind of spirits.

One other method of arresting fermentation, in order to retain the sweetness in wine, is pasteurization, the same method used in dairies to protect milk.

These "sweet" wines include the "appetizer wines," such as Sherry and Vermouth, and also the "dessert wines," such as Port, Muscatel, and Tokay. These wines, as the names suggest, are customarily served, before dinner as appetizers, or for dessert and refreshment.

The alcohol content of such wines is about 20 per cent by volume.

SPARKLING WINES

The sparkling wines are the light, effervescent wines, both red and white. They sparkle because of a secondary fermentation of the wine, which takes place either in the bottle or in large glass-lined containers. A fine sparkling wine must be handled hundreds of times and requires special bottles and corks. This extensive handling and care in bottling explain why sparkling wines cost more than other wines.

Sparkling wines are all-occasion wines. They may be served before dinner, during or after meals, or for refreshment. The best known of the sparkling wines are Champagne and Sparkling Burgundy.

WINE NAMES

As there are hundreds of different names for different wines, not even a professional winetaster knows them all. The important fact is that there are only five principal *classes* of wines, and virtually all wines fit into one of these groups:

1. The appetizer wines
2. The white table wines
3. The red table wines
4. The dessert wines
5. The sparkling wines

In these five classes are twelve internationally known wine *types*. If you can recognize these you may consider yourself ably informed about wines. Here they are, set up in comprehensive chart form, together with a taste-and-color description:

THE TWELVE PRINCIPAL WINE TYPES

Appetizer Wines

SHERRY—a wine characterized by a distinctive nutlike flavor, ranging in color from pale to dark amber. Sherries range in taste from sweet to very dry.

VERMOUTH—a wine flavored with aromatic herbs. There are two types: (1) a dry Vermouth, sometimes identified as French-type Vermouth, and (2) a sweet Vermouth, also known as Italian-type Vermouth.

White Table Wines

SAUTERNE—a golden, full-bodied wine of piquant flavor.

RHINE WINE—a delicate light wine of pale golden color.

Red Table Wines

CLARET—a fragrant red medium-bodied wine with tasty sharpness. Clarets are considered the leading mealtime wines in most parts of the world.

BURGUNDY—a dark, ruby-red wine, slightly heartier in flavor, body, and bouquet than Claret.

Dessert Wines

PORT—a fruity sweet wine, ranging from deep red to tawny color.

MUSCATEL—a wine with the distinctive flavor, aroma, and sweetness of Muscat grapes.

TOKAY—an amber-colored wine whose sweetness is midway between that of Sherry and Port.

WHITE PORT—a straw-colored wine, said to have been produced first for sacramental use.

Sparkling Wines

CHAMPAGNE—a light, choice white wine, made sparkling by the Champagne process—a secondary fermentation which creates a natural effervescence. Champagne may be dry (*brut*), semi-dry (usually labeled "dry"), and sweet (*doux*).

SPARKLING BURGUNDY—a smooth, choice red wine, made naturally sparkling by the same process as Champagne.

MORE ABOUT WINE NAMES

For those of you who wish to delve more deeply into wine lore, the following chart will take you on to the next step. Repeated here are the five basic classes of wines and the twelve principal wine types shown on the preceding chart. Then, grouped with each wine type or "wine family" are the seventy-two wine names most frequently applied to wines in America.

For example, under Red Table Wines are listed the two principal wine types—Claret and Burgundy. Also listed are additional members of the Claret and Burgundy types or "families," which are known by other names to indicate varying shades of richness, color, and flavor.

To illustrate this you will note that Zinfandel is shown in the Red Table Wine class. Zinfandel is a member of the Claret type, but this wine has its own name which identifies its distinctive Zinfandel grape flavor and fragrance.

Cabernet is another Red Table Wine of the Claret type or "family," but it is named after the Cabernet grapes from which it is made and which give this wine its individual, characteristic fruity taste and aroma.

In similar fashion there is the White Table Wine group, with its two principal types—Sauterne and Rhine Wine—and additional members of these two wine "families." Thus, Chablis belongs to the Rhine Wine family, but usually has a slightly more fruity flavor than Rhine Wine. Riesling is another Rhine Wine type, with the characteristic flavor of the Riesling grapes from which it is made.

The 72 Type Names Most Frequently Applied to Wine in the United States

Appetizer Wines

SHERRY	Madeira
VERMOUTH	Marsala

Red Table Wines

CLARET	Aleatico
BURGUNDY	Barbera

Barberone
Cabernet
Carignane
Charbono
Chianti
Concord
Duriff
Gamay
Grignolino
Ives
Mourestel
Norton
Petite Sirah
Pinot Noir
Rose
Zinfandel

White Table Wines

RHINE WINE
SAUTERNE
Catawba
Chablis
Chardonnay
Château Sauterne
Delaware
Dry Sauterne
Elvira
Folle Blanche
Golden Chasselas
Gutedel
Haut Sauterne
Hock
Light Muscat
Malvasia Bianca
Mascato Canelli
Moselle
Muscat Frontignan
Pinot Blanc
Riesling
Sauvignon Blanc
Scuppernong
Semillon
Sweet Sauterne
Sylvaner
Traminer
Ugni-Blanc
White Chianti

Dessert Wines

MUSCATEL
PORT
TOKAY
WHITE PORT
Aleatico
Angelica
Malaga
Malvasia
Muscat Frontignon
Red Muscatel
Sweet Sherry

Sparkling Wines

CHAMPAGNE	Pink Champagne
SPARKLING BURGUNDY	Sparkling Mascato
Canelli	Sparkling Moselle
Mascato Spumante	Sparkling Muscat
	Sparkling Sauterne

CHAPTER 3

WINE SERVICE GUIDE, TEMPERATURES, TABLE SERVICE, AND WINE GLASSWARE

Wine is the most healthful and most hygienic of beverages.

LOUIS PASTEUR

There are certain customs or conventions which have grown up about serving wine, just as there are conventions about serving foods. Corned beef with cabbage is a familiar food custom or convention, as is turkey with cranberry sauce and liver with bacon. Such conventions have developed because many people found they enjoyed these particular flavor combinations, and gradually the combinations became customary.

It is the same with wine. Most people enjoy the taste and flavor of the full-bodied red table wines, such as Claret and Burgundy, combined with the flavors of hearty red meats. There is, similarly, a popular preference for the light and delicate white table wines, Sauterne and Rhine Wine, with the more delicately flavored white meats, such as chicken or seafood. But these are popular preferences, not rules; and you will soon discover the wine-and-food flavor combinations which please your own palate.

Each wine has its own individual, characteristic flavor: the flavor and taste of Sauterne differs from that of Rhine Wine; Claret has a flavor different from that of Burgundy; Sherry has a distinctive flavor all its own.

You'll want to try the taste and flavors of different wines until you discover your own special favorites. Meantime we offer the following guide for ready reference:

BEFORE DINNER

The appetizer wines, Sherry and Vermouth, are appropriate as an inviting before-dinner cocktail. These versatile wines may also be offered for refreshment during the afternoon or evening. Madeira and Marsala are two other well-known before-dinner wines. Serve cool.

WITH DINNER

The red table wines, Claret and Burgundy, taste especially good with red meats such as steaks, hamburger, roasts, game, and venison. Other popular red table wines are Zinfandel, Chianti, Cabernet. Serve cool.

The white table wines, Sauterne and Rhine Wine, are an excellent choice with chicken or seafood. Chablis, Moselle, Riesling, and Hock are other popular white table wines. Serve lightly chilled.

AFTER DINNER

The dessert wines, Port, Muscatel, and Tokay, may be offered as your dessert course, with cheese and crackers, or fruit. These wines are ideal to serve for refreshment, afternoon or evening. Serve cool.

SPARKLING WINES

The sparkling wines, Champagne and Sparkling Burgundy, are all-occasion, all-purpose wines, and may be appropriately offered before dinner, with foods, and for afternoon or evening refreshment. Serve thoroughly iced.

TEMPERATURES FOR SERVING WINE

The oft-heard phrase "serve wine at room temperature" has come down to us from olden times when, in European countries, wines were stored in deep, cool, underground cellars, then transported and served in dining rooms which were generally unheated. Thus, in reality, "room temperature" was apt to be cool. In modern times, here in America, "room temperature" can be misleading, as you'll agree if you compare the temperature in a steam-heated apartment with that of a flat or a house. A better general rule to follow is to serve wine cool or lightly chilled. In other words, place your wine in the refrigerator for one to three hours before serving.

The sole exception to this general rule are the sparkling wines, Champagne and Sparkling Burgundy; these wines are always served thoroughly iced.

POURING THE WINE

Table wines, both red and white, are usually served from the bottle.

Sherry and Vermouth, and other appetizer wines, may be served from the bottle or a decanter when offered before dinner as a cocktail, or in the evening for refreshment.

Port, Muscatel, and Tokay, and other dessert wines, may also be served from the bottle or a decanter.

Wineglasses should be filled only three fourths full. In that way you can enjoy all the fine, full fragrance and bouquet of the wine as well as its delicious taste. Do not lift glasses when filling.

INFORMAL TABLE SERVICE

It is customary today to serve only one wine with luncheons or informal dinners. This may be a red table wine, such as Claret or Burgundy, or one of the white table wines, Sauterne or Rhine Wine.

The wine is poured with the first course of the dinner, and it is permissible to allow the bottle to remain on the table.

The wineglass is placed on the table to the right of the water glass, and usually on a line with the water glass.

FORMAL TABLE SERVICE

On formal occasions, when you wish to offer different wines with various courses of the meal, the wines are usually served like this:

With hors d'oeuvres	—*Sherry or Champagne*
With soup	—*Sherry*
With fish	—*A white table wine, such as Sauterne or Rhine Wine*
With entrée	—*A second table wine, either red or white*
With dessert	—*A dessert wine, such as Port, Muscatel, or Tokay*

For elaborate dinners, no more than two wineglasses are on the table at any time. The water goblet is on a line with the knife, and the wineglasses may be set to the right of the water goblet.

Wineglasses for any additional wines are exchanged as each course is finished and the next one served.

CHOICE OF WINE GLASSWARE

The shape of the glass in which you serve wine is entirely a matter of personal taste. Most people, however, prefer stemmed glasses, which show off the lovely colors of the wines and lend additional beauty to your table settings.

The amount of wine ordinarily served per glass is worthy of note, so follow this simple formula for appropriate servings:

	SUGGESTED SIZE OF GLASS
Sherry and Vermouth, or any appetizer wine	2 to 3 ounces
Claret, Burgundy, or any red table wine	5 to 7 ounces
Sauterne, Rhine Wine, or any white table wine	5 to 7 ounces
Port, Muscatel, Tokay, or any dessert wine	2 to 3 ounces
Champagne, Sparkling Burgundy, and other sparkling wines are usually served in a saucer-type glass—a champagne goblet or wide-brimmed sherbet glass	4 to 5 ounces

Since today's hospitality stresses simplicity, it is no longer essential to have a vast array of glassware for serving wines. For practical, all-around service we suggest a basic glass wardrobe containing:

1—a glass holding 2 to 3 ounces, usually described as a Sherry glass, for serving Sherry, Vermouth, Port, Muscatel, or Tokay.

2—a glass holding 5 to 7 ounces, usually described as a Claret glass, for serving any of the red or white table wines. A stemmed water goblet could serve this purpose since it holds just about the right amount.

3—a stemmed, wide-brimmed sherbet glass, for serving Champagne and Sparkling Burgundy, which may also be used as a fruit cocktail or dessert dish.

CHAPTER 4

HELPFUL HINTS ABOUT WINE BUYING, WINE CARE, AND WINE STORING

A day without wine is a day without sunshine.

OLD FRENCH PROVERB

WHAT AMOUNT OF WINE TO BUY

One bottle (four-fifths quart) of red or white table wine (Claret, Burgundy, Sauterne, Rhine Wine) will serve eight glasses.

The appetizer wines, Sherry and Vermouth, are offered in smaller portions, and a bottle (four-fifths quart) provides approximately sixteen servings. This is likewise true of the dessert wines, such as Port, Muscatel, and Tokay.

The sparkling wines, such as Champagne and Sparkling Burgundy, are usually sold in bottles containing 24 to 26 ounces, which will serve eight.

ARE WINES PERISHABLE?

The red table wines, such as Claret and Burgundy, and the white table wines, Sauterne and Rhine Wine, are perishable. These table wines will usually keep for only two to three days after being opened. Once opened, keep them in the refrigerator and use as quickly as possible.

The appetizer wines, such as Sherry and Vermouth,

will keep indefinitely, even after being opened as will the dessert wines such as Port, Muscatel and Tokay.

WHAT WINES TO BUY

A small, selected stock of wines will keep you prepared for any occasion, and a well-balanced, inexpensive "wine cellar" might include:

Two to three bottles of red table wines, Claret or Burgundy.
Two to three bottles of white table wines, Sauterne or Rhine Wine.
One bottle of Sherry, for service as an appetizer or for refreshment.
One bottle of Port for dessert service, or for refreshment.

HOW TO STORE WINES IN YOUR HOME

Store wines away from sunlight, preferably in a cool place.

If the wines are corked, the bottles should be kept lying on their sides. This is especially important in the care of the sparkling wines, such as Champagne and Sparkling Burgundy.

If wine bottles are capped, they may stand upright.

CHAPTER *5*

SOUPS

Nothing more excellent or valuable than wine was ever granted by the Gods to man.

PLATO

Every cook will agree, I think, that in soups the flavor is of prime importance. One of the simplest ways to heighten the flavor of soups is to add a measure of fragrant wine, for wine has a natural affinity with soups. Whether your favorite soup be clear or creamy, whether you serve it hot or cold, in a cup or a full, generous bowl, a tablespoon or two of wine will lend appetizing new goodness and palatability.

As in all cooking, wine is used in soups as a seasoning and, since wine should be heated, but not boiled, the wine is added just before removing the soup from the stove.

Favorite wine-and-soup flavor combinations are Sherry with cream or clear soups or French onion soup; Sauterne, Rhine Wine or any of the white table wines in chowder or consommé; Claret, Burgundy, or any of the red table wines in clear tomato or vegetable soup.

Usual proportions are one to two tablespoons per portion, and it's a good rule to add a little less rather than a little more.

CONSOMMÉ, BURGUNDY (*Serves 8*)

½ cup cooked macaroni or spaghetti
2 cans strong consommé or bouillon
Celery salt
¼ cup Burgundy or Claret
Grated Parmesan cheese

Cut macaroni or spaghetti in half-inch lengths and heat in soup. Add celery salt to taste. When boiling point is reached, add wine and remove from heat. Serve immediately, with dusting of cheese.

TOMATO BOUILLON, CLARET (*Serves 4*)

1 pint tomato juice
2 bouillon cubes
½ cup Claret or Burgundy
Celery tops
1 small onion, diced
3 whole cloves
1 bay leaf
Salt and pepper

To the tomato juice add a few celery tops, onion, bay leaf, cloves, and salt and pepper to taste. Simmer for 20 to 30 minutes. Strain. Dissolve bouillon cubes in hot liquid. Add wine, bring to boiling, and serve at once with a thin slice of lemon in each cup.

FRENCH ONION SOUP (*Serves 4 to 6*)

6 medium-sized onions, sliced
¼ cup butter or margarine
5 cups boiling water and 5 bouillon cubes or
5 cups beef or chicken broth
3 slices bread
Salt and pepper
1 cup Sherry
½ cup grated cheese

Sauté the onions slowly in the butter or margarine until golden brown. Add the hot bouillon (or broth) and simmer for 20 minutes. Toast the bread on both sides. Spread with butter and cut into quarters. Season soup to taste with salt and pepper, and add Sherry. Pour into individual casseroles, or one large casserole, and top with toast sprinkled generously with grated cheese. Place casserole in hot oven until grated cheese browns slightly—about 10 minutes.

WINE GIBLET SOUP (*Serves 4*)

- Livers, hearts, and gizzards of 2 chickens or 1 turkey
- ¼ cup butter or margarine
- 4 cups chicken broth
- ¼ cup celery, chopped
- 4 sprigs parsley
- Salt and pepper
- ½ cup Sherry

Cover the gizzards and hearts with cold water and cook slowly for half an hour. Drain and cut in small pieces. Cut liver in small pieces. Brown the giblets in butter. Heat chicken stock with celery and parsley. Add the fried giblets and cook slowly for about 20 minutes. Strain through coarse sieve, forcing the liver through the sieve. Season with salt and pepper to taste. Add the Sherry. Reheat and serve.

BLACK BEAN SOUP (*Serves 8*)

- 2 cups black beans
- 2 qts. water
- ¼ lb. raw ham or salt pork
- 1 cup celery, chopped
- 2 onions, minced
- 1 tsp. salt
- 6 peppercorns
- 4 whole cloves
- ¼ tsp. mustard
- 1 bay leaf
- 2 tbsps. flour
- 2 tbsps. butter or margarine
- ⅓ cup Sherry
- Hard-cooked eggs, sliced
- Lemon slices

Soak the beans in cold water overnight. Drain and place in large kettle. Add the 2 quarts of water. Cut the meat in cubes and add. Add celery, onions, salt, peppercorns, cloves, mustard, and bay leaf. Cover and cook gently for 2½ hours. Strain the soup, reserving the cubes of meat. Blend flour with butter or margarine and add to hot soup. Cook, stirring constantly, until soup is slightly thickened. Add meat cubes, Sherry. Heat thoroughly. Serve garnished with sliced hard-cooked eggs and lemon slices.

MOCK-TURTLE SOUP WITH SHERRY (*Serves 4*)

1 can condensed mock-turtle soup
½ can water
3 tbsps. Sherry

Heat soup and water in saucepan. Remove from heat and add Sherry just before serving. Float a thin slice of lemon on each serving.

TOMATO SOUP SHERRY (*Serves 4*)

1 can tomato soup
1 can water
½ cup Sherry

Add water to soup and heat to boiling. Add Sherry, heat (but do not boil), and serve with lemon slices.

MUSHROOM SOUP WITH SHERRY (*Serves 3 to 4*)

1 10½ oz. can condensed mushroom soup
1 cup milk
3 tbsps. Sherry

Blend soup and milk, and heat slowly to simmering. Just before serving, stir in Sherry. If homemade or ready-to-serve canned cream of mushroom soup is used instead of condensed, simply add 1½ tablespoons Sherry for each cup of undiluted soup.

BORSCH (*Serves 6*)

- 1 soup bone or 1 lb. short ribs
- ½ lb. stewing beef
- 3 qts. water
- 3 medium onions, sliced
- ⅓ cup celery, chopped
- 1 green pepper, chopped
- 2 cups cabbage, shredded
- 3 tomatoes, cut in pieces
- 3 cups cooked beets, grated
- 1 cup Sauterne or Rhine Wine
- Salt and pepper
- ½ pt. sour cream

Cook soup bone or short ribs, beef, and onions in 3 quarts boiling water for 2 hours. Add celery, pepper, cabbage, and tomatoes and cook for 10 minutes. Then add beets and wine. Simmer for 5 minutes. Serve hot. Top each serving with a generous spoonful of whipped sour cream.

CREAM OF POTATO SOUP, SAUTERNE (*Serves 4 to 6*)

- 8 medium potatoes
- ¼ lb. bacon, cut in pieces
- 3 small onions, minced
- 2½ tsps. salt
- ¼ tsp. pepper
- 2 cups potato water
- ¾ cup Sauterne or Rhine Wine
- 1½ cups light cream
- Parsley, chopped

Peel and dice the potatoes. Cover with water and cook until done. Drain potato water, reserving 2 cups of the liquid. Mash potatoes well. Fry the bacon. Remove cubes of bacon and brown onions in hot bacon fat. Add potatoes, potato water, and fried bacon cubes. Season with salt and pepper. Add the wine and cream. Simmer for 5 minutes. Serve garnished with parsley and croutons.

FISH CHOWDER, SAUTERNE (*Serves 6 to 8*)

- 3 tbsps. butter or margarine
- 4 tbsps. minced onion
- 1 small can shrimp, chopped
- 1 small can minced clams
- 1 can mixed vegetables, drained
- 2 cups medium white sauce
- Salt and pepper
- ½ cup Sauterne or Rhine Wine

Melt butter or margarine in frying pan. Add onion, shrimp, minced clams, and vegetables. Sauté together for 5 minutes. Make white sauce in usual way. Just before serving combine the two mixtures, season to taste, and stir in wine.

SHRIMP BISQUE (*Serves 5 to 6*)

- 2 cups cooked or canned shrimp
- ½ cup Sauterne or Rhine Wine
- ¼ cup butter, margarine, or cooking oil
- ¼ cup flour
- 1 tbsp. onion, minced
- 3 cups milk
- Salt and pepper
- 1 cup cream
- Dash cayenne

Add the wine to the shrimp, cover, and set in the refrigerator for half an hour. Prepare white sauce as follows: Melt butter, margarine, or cooking oil in top of double boiler. Add the flour gradually and blend until smooth. Cook for 2 to 3 minutes. Scald the milk, add the minced onion, and stir into butter-flour mixture.

Cook, stirring constantly, until thickened and smooth. Season with salt and pepper. Add the shrimp and the wine. Add the cream. Heat thoroughly. Add a dash of cayenne. Serve with croutons.

POTATO CHOWDER (*Serves 5*)

3 cups diced raw potatoes
1½ cups diced raw carrots
1 small onion, minced
2 cups boiling water
1½ tsps. salt
2 cups milk
½ cup Sauterne or Rhine Wine
Pepper
Celery salt

Cook potatoes, carrots, and onion in boiling salted water until very tender. Do not drain. Mash slightly, add milk. Season to taste with salt, pepper, celery salt, and heat to boiling. Add wine and serve at once, sprinkling each serving with minced parsley.

WHITE WINE SOUP (*Serves 4*)

2 tbsps. butter or margarine
2 tbsps. flour
1 pint apple or peach juice
1 inch stick cinnamon
6 tbsps. sugar
4 twists of lemon peel or 4 lemon slices
2 eggs, separated
2 cups Sauterne or Rhine Wine

Melt the butter or margarine and add flour. Bring apple or peach juice to a boil and add to flour mixture gradually, stirring until smooth. Return to saucepan. Add cinnamon, 2 tablespoons of sugar, and the lemon peel. Cook 5 minutes, stirring constantly, until thickened and smooth. Add the wine. Heat thoroughly. Beat egg yolks until thick. Add hot mixture to egg yolks gradually, return to saucepan, and cook for one minute. Beat egg whites until stiff. Add remaining sugar. Drop by spoonfuls on the hot soup. Serve immediately or chill thoroughly.

SPLIT PEA SOUP (*Serves 6*)

1¼ cups green split peas
1 cup celery, chopped
2 onions, chopped
1 tbsp. salt
1 bay leaf
6 cups water
2 bouillon cubes
¾ cup milk
¾ cup Sauterne or Rhine Wine

Soak the peas for 4 hours, or overnight. Drain. Put peas, celery, onions, salt, and bay leaf into soup kettle. Add the water, cover, and simmer for 2 hours. Stir in the bouillon cubes, milk, and wine. Serve very hot, topping each portion with croutons.

OLD-FASHIONED BEAN SOUP (*Serves 8 to 10*)

1 pint dry beans
2 qts. water
2 tsps. salt
1 medium onion
2 tbsps. butter or margarine
1 ham bone or 4 strips of bacon
2 cups tomatoes, canned or fresh
1 tsp. sugar
1 tbsp. flour
¾ cup Claret or Burgundy

Soak beans overnight in water to cover. Drain, and add the 2 quarts of water and the salt. Sauté the onion in the butter or margarine and add to the beans. Add the ham bone, or bacon cut in cubes. Cook slowly in a covered kettle for approximately 3 hours, or until beans are soft and the skins can be blown loose. Add more water as needed. Add the tomatoes, sugar, and the flour which has been blended with 2 tablespoons of soup. Cook for 15 minutes. Add the wine immediately before serving.

RHUBARB WINE SOUP (*Serves 6*)

1 tbsp. cornstarch
¾ cup sugar
1 cup water
2 inches stick cinnamon
¼ tsp. mace
¼ tsp. nutmeg
3 slices lemon
2 cups Claret or Burgundy
2 cups rhubarb, cut fine

Combine cornstarch and sugar. Add water and cook, stirring constantly, until mixture is thickened and smooth. Add spices, lemon slices, wine, and rhubarb. Simmer for 5 minutes. Serve piping hot, or well chilled, accompanied by water crackers when served as an appetizer and with vanilla wafers when featured as dessert.

CHAPTER *6*

SALADS AND SALAD DRESSINGS

Wine is as old as civilization, and no drink except water and milk has won such universal commendation through the ages. It is used to perform rites in churches; to observe memorable occasions; to launch ships; to minister to the sick; to welcome guests; to inspire the mind. It is essentially a drink of moderation; when used to excess, wine itself is abused.

ENCYCLOPAEDIA BRITANNICA

FROZEN SHERRY JELLY SALAD

(*Serves 8*)

2 tbsps. gelatin
½ cup cold water
¾ cup boiling water
½ cup sugar
1¼ cups orange juice
¼ cup lemon juice
1 cup Sherry
Dash of salt

Soak gelatin in cold water. Dissolve in boiling water. Add sugar. Stir until dissolved. Add strained orange juice and lemon juice, Sherry, and dash of salt. Pour into mold. Chill until firm. Unmold. Serve with fruits on large salad tray. May be served with Sherry Cream Dressing.

Sherry Cream Dressing for Fruit Salad (*Serves 8*)

⅓ cup Sherry
Juice and rind of 2 lemons
Whipping cream, whipped
½ cup sugar
2 eggs, eggs and whites beaten separately

Combine Sherry, lemon juice, and rind, ¼ cup of the sugar, and beaten egg yolks. Cook over hot water until thickened. Add remaining ¼ cup sugar to the beaten egg whites. Fold into hot mixture. Continue cooking over hot water for about 10 minutes. Stir constantly. Chill. When ready to serve, fold in whipping cream to suit the taste.

FRUIT SALAD, SHERRY HONEY DRESSING
(*Serves 6*)

3 oranges, sliced
6 apricots, cooked and halved
3 pears, cooked and halved
1 cup sweet cherries, pitted
1 cup raspberries or blackberries
1 bunch water cress
½ cup Sherry
¼ cup honey
Juice of 1 lemon

Arrange fruits on one large salad plate or on individual plates, as desired. Serve with Sherry dressing made by blending wine with honey and lemon juice. A rotary beater may be used to blend the dressing ingredients.

SHERRY GRAPEFRUIT SALAD RING
(*Serves 8 to 12*)

2 or 3 grapefruit
2 tbsps. unflavored gelatin
½ cup cold water
2 cups boiling water and grapefruit juice
½ cup honey
Few grains salt
¾ cup Sherry
¼ cup lemon juice

Pare grapefruit. Remove outer membrane. Slip out sections, saving juice. Add water to make 2 cups, and heat to boiling. Soak gelatin in cold water for 5 minutes, then dissolve in boiling water and grapefruit juice. Add rest of ingredients, and cool. When mixture begins to stiffen, fold in grapefruit sections. Pour into ring mold and chill.

FROZEN FRUIT SALAD *(Serves 8 to 10)*

- 2 tbsps. unflavored gelatin
- ½ cup cold water
- 1½ cups boiling water
- ¾ cup sugar or honey
- ½ cup strained orange juice
- 3 tbsps. strained lemon juice
- 1¼ cups Port or Sherry
- Few grains salt

Soften gelatin in cold water. Add boiling water and sugar or honey. Stir until dissolved. Add other ingredients, pour into mold, and chill. Unmold on serving dish and garnish with fruit, if desired. This salad may also be served as dessert, topped with custard sauce.

GREEN BEAN SALAD, WHITE WINE
(Serves 6)

- 1 qt. green beans, cut in pieces
- 3 slices bacon, cut in small pieces
- 1 onion, sliced
- ¾ cup Sauterne or Rhine Wine
- 3 tbsps. sugar
- 3 tbsps. vinegar
- 2 tsps. cornstarch
- 2 tbsps. water

Cover beans with boiling water. Cook, uncovered, for about 20 minutes, or until just tender. Add 1 scant teaspoon salt after first 10 minutes of cooking. Drain. Fry bacon pieces until crisp. Add to beans. Cook onion in bacon fat for 3 minutes. Add onion to beans. Add wine, sugar, and vinegar to bacon fat. Dissolve cornstarch in cold water. Add to wine sauce. Cook, stirring constantly, until slightly thickened and clear. Mix dressing, bacon bits, and onion through beans. Serve warm.

CRANBERRY SALAD MOLD (*Serves 8 to 10*)

- 2 packages raspberry gelatin
- 1½ cups hot water
- 2 cups Burgundy or Claret
- 1½ cups cranberry sauce, sweetened

Dissolve gelatin in hot water. Cool. Add the wine. Allow to congeal slightly, then add the cranberry sauce. Pour into mold which has been rinsed in cold water, place in refrigerator, and chill until firm.

WHITE WINE POTATO SALAD (*Serves 6*)

- 4 large potatoes, or
- 8 small new potatoes
- ½ cup Sauterne or Rhine Wine
- ¼ cup salad oil
- 3 tbsps. vinegar
- 1 tbsp. sugar
- 3 tbsps. onion, chopped
- Salt and pepper

Boil potatoes in jackets until done. Peel and slice into bowl while still warm. Moisten thoroughly with the wine. Add other ingredients. Allow to stand in a cool place for at least 1 hour before serving.

GARDEN SALAD, BURGUNDY (*Serves 6*)

- 1 head lettuce
- 2 tomatoes, cut in eighths
- 1 stalk celery, cut in strips
- 3 carrots, cut in strips
- 2 green onions, sliced
- ½ unpeeled cucumber, sliced thin
- Water cress
- ½ cup salad oil
- 2 tbsps. lemon juice
- 1 tbsp. sugar
- ½ tsp. salt
- ⅛ tsp. pepper
- ½ cup Burgundy or Claret

Cut lettuce and tomatoes into bowl. Add celery, carrots, onions, cucumber, and water cress. Mix salad oil through salad before bringing to the table. Blend lemon juice, salt, pepper, and wine in small bowl at table. Pour over salad, toss lightly, and serve.

CHICKEN SALAD, WHITE WINE (*Serves 6*)

2 cups cooked chicken, cut in pieces
Salt, pepper, and thyme
½ cup Sauterne or Rhine Wine
1 tablespoon lemon juice
1½ cups celery, chopped
½ cup walnut meats
½ cup boiled salad dressing
Tomatoes, carrot sticks, lettuce

Season chicken with salt, pepper, and thyme. Transfer to shallow refrigerator dish. Pour wine and lemon juice over chicken. Cover, and allow to stand in wine marinade for 3 or 4 hours. Remove chicken from marinade.

Combine chicken, celery, and nut meats. Add small amounts of leftover wine marinade to boiled dressing and beat with rotary beater. Continue to add wine to dressing until dressing is the consistency of rather thick cream. Toss dressing through salad. Arrange in lettuce cup. Garnish platter with tomatoes and carrot sticks.

HAM SALAD MOLD (*Serves 6 to 8*)

2 tbsps. unflavored gelatin
2 cups ham, cubed
½ cup cold water
3 cups broth, heated
Salt
½ cup Claret or Burgundy
1 cup fresh green peas, cooked
Mayonnaise
Mint leaves

Soak gelatin in cold water. Dissolve in hot broth. Add salt to taste. Cool, and add wine. Place in refrigerator and chill until mixture thickens slightly. Pour ½ cup of this gelatin mixture into bottom of a ring mold which has been rinsed in cold water. Chill until it begins to congeal. Then arrange a layer of ham cubes and green peas on the gelatin layer. Add remaining ham and peas to remaining gelatin mixture. Pour over first layer. Chill until firm. Unmold, and serve with mayonnaise and a garnish of mint leaves if desired.

SALMON SALAD, SAUTERNE (*Serves 4*)

2 cups canned salmon
¼ cup Sauterne or Rhine Wine
1 small onion, minced
½ cup celery, diced
2 tbsps. lemon juice
Salt, celery salt, and pepper
⅓ cup mayonnaise

Drain and flake the salmon. Add wine and seasonings. Combine with mayonnaise and serve.

WINE FRENCH DRESSING (*1½ cups*)

1 tbsp. sugar
1 tsp. salt
½ tsp. dry mustard
1 tsp. Worcestershire sauce
4 tbsps. catsup
4 tbsps. Claret or Burgundy
4 tbsps. wine vinegar
¾ cup salad oil
1 clove garlic, crushed

Combine all ingredients in order given in a pint or quart jar, and shake until thoroughly mixed. This dressing may be kept indefinitely in your refrigerator, but you may wish to remove garlic after a day or two. Always shake well before using.

WINE ROQUEFORT DRESSING

(1/3 cup dressing. Serves 3 to 4)

- 1 small pkg. Roquefort-type cheese (1 1/4 oz.)
- 1/4 cup salad oil
- 2 tbsps. wine vinegar
- Salt and black pepper to taste
- 2 tbsps. Claret or Burgundy
- 1/2 tsp. Worcestershire sauce

Mash cheese with a fork, blend in oil, vinegar, and wine. Add seasonings to taste. Especially good on lettuce or mixed greens, tomatoes, or grapefruit.

CHAPTER 7

VEGETABLES, EGG AND CHEESE DISHES

Drink no longer water, but use a little wine for thy stomach's sake.

1 TIMOTHY, CH. 5, V. 23 (*New Testament*)

Sherry is traditionally favored with cheese and egg dishes, and the light, white table wines, such as Sauterne and Rhine Wine, are next in popularity. In the preparation of vegetables and meatless dishes the red and white table wines, Sherry or the sweeter wines, such as Port, may be successfully used to improve the flavor of the foods, or to high light the sauce or dressing. The white table wines are recommended for combining with carrots, artichokes, and other vegetables light in color and delicate in flavor; the red table wines are usually preferred with kidney-bean dishes, baked beans, spaghetti, or macaroni.

WINE BUTTER SAUCE FOR VEGETABLES

3 egg yolks
⅓ cup water
3 tbsps. Sauterne or Rhine Wine
1 tbsp. lemon juice
Salt, pepper
½ cup butter

Beat egg yolks until light. Add water, wine, lemon juice, salt and pepper to taste to the beaten egg yolks.

Cook slowly in a double boiler until thick, stirring frequently. Add the butter slowly, beating thoroughly, until all has been added. Serve hot.

SAUTERNE HOLLANDAISE SAUCE

¾ cup butter
1 tbsp. lemon juice
¼ tsp. salt
¼ cup Sauterne or Rhine Wine
3 egg yolks, well beaten
⅛ tsp. pepper
¼ cup boiling water

Place ¼ cup butter in top of double boiler. Add well-beaten egg yolks to which lemon juice and wine have been added. Heat slowly, stirring constantly. When the first ¼ cup butter has melted, add second ¼ cup butter, beating all the while. Finally, when second portion butter has melted, add remaining butter. Cook until sauce is thickened, beating constantly. Add boiling water slowly one minute before removing from hot water. Add salt and pepper. Serve with fresh green vegetables.

ARTICHOKES IN RHINE WINE (*Serves 6*)

6 small artichokes
1 onion, minced
1 clove garlic, minced
2 tsps. salt
1 tbsp. cooking oil
1 cup Rhine Wine or Sauterne

Place artichokes upright in pot. Add onion, garlic, and salt. Pour cooking oil and wine over all, cover tightly, and allow to simmer very slowly. Add more wine as moisture evaporates. Cook for 45 minutes, or until hearts are tender.

BAKED BEANS, RED WINE (*Serves 4*)

6 to 8 slices bacon
1 onion, sliced
½ cup Claret or Burgundy
1 large can baked beans

Fry bacon until partly done, not crisp. Take up bacon and pour off all but about 2 tablespoons of the fat. Add sliced onion and fry gently 5 minutes in the hot fat. Then add wine and beans. Mix thoroughly. Pour into a shallow casserole and bake in a moderately hot oven (400 degrees F.) for about 20 minutes, until bubbly. Top with partly cooked bacon slices and put back in oven until bacon is crisp.

KIDNEY-BEAN CASSEROLE (*Serves 6*)

4 cups kidney beans, canned
1 cup Claret or Burgundy
2 tbsps. butter or margarine
2 tbsps. flour
2 tbsps. parsley, minced
½ pound ground beef
1 medium onion, sliced
¼ cup green pepper, chopped
Salt and pepper
Butter or fat for browning beef

Drain kidney beans, reserving the liquid. Add wine to liquid from kidney beans and heat. Add flour which has been blended with 2 tablespoons butter or margarine. Cook, stirring constantly, until mixture is smooth and thick. Form the beef into tiny balls and brown beef, onion, and green pepper in butter or other cooking fat. Add the wine gravy and the parsley. Add salt and pepper to taste. Arrange kidney beans in a casserole and pour wine sauce and meat balls over beans. Bake in a 350-degree oven for about 30 minutes. Serve with crisp green salad.

SHERRIED BAKED BEANS (*Serves 6 to 8*)

2 lbs. navy beans
½ lb. ham, cut in cubes
2 tsps. salt
2 tbsps. brown sugar
½ cup molasses
2 cups Sherry

Soak navy beans in water overnight. Drain, cover with fresh boiling water, and cook over low flame until skins begin to break. Combine ham with beans and place in bean pot. Add 1 cup hot water. Place salt, brown sugar, and molasses over top of beans and bake in very slow oven for 6 hours. Add small amounts of the wine to the beans at intervals to keep beans almost covered with liquid at all times. After the first 6 hours of baking add remaining wine and bake 1 hour longer at a slightly higher temperature.

GREEN CABBAGE SAUTERNE (*Serves 4*)

4 frankfurters
¼ cup butter or margarine
1 large onion
¾ cup Sauterne or Rhine Wine
2 tbsps. sugar
1 tbsp. flour
½ tsp. salt
¼ tsp. pepper
2 cups cabbage, shredded

Split frankfurters and sauté in butter or margarine until lightly browned. Remove to hot platter. Sauté onion until yellow. Combine wine, sugar, flour, salt and pepper in small covered jar and shake vigorously until well blended. Add to onions in skillet and cook, stirring constantly, until smooth and slightly thickened. Add cabbage and cook, stirring constantly, with wine dressing for about 6 minutes. Serve topped with sautéed frankfurters and garnish with green onions.

SHERRIED LIMA BEANS (*Serves 4 to 6*)

2 strips bacon, or 3 tbsps. meat fryings
1 onion, chopped
2 medium-sized ripe tomatoes, diced
3 tbsps. brown sugar
2 tbsps. vinegar
¾ cup Sherry
4 cups drained, cooked dry Lima beans
Salt, pepper

Cut bacon fine and fry crisp, or melt meat fryings. Add chopped onion and fry until limp. Add brown sugar, diced tomatoes, and vinegar, and simmer for 10 minutes. Add Sherry and beans; salt and pepper to taste. Heat thoroughly, and serve. Or place in casserole and bake in moderate oven (350 degrees F.) for 30 minutes.

BEETS IN PORT (*Serves 4*)

2 cups diced cooked beets
½ cup beet liquid or water
½ cup Port
1 tbsp. sugar
2 tsps. cornstarch
1 tsp. butter or margarine

Heat beet liquid or water and wine; add sugar mixed with cornstarch and cook, stirring until transparent. Add beets, butter or margarine, and salt and pepper to taste. Heat thoroughly.

RED CABBAGE IN WINE (*Serves 6*)

1 cup Claret or Burgundy
1 cup boiling water
1 head red cabbage, shredded
3 cooking apples, sliced
1 tsp. salt
2 small onions, minced
¼ cup sugar
1 tbsp. butter or margarine
2 tbsps. flour

Add wine to boiling water and bring to a full boil. Add the shredded cabbage, apples, salt, and onions. Cook for about 20 minutes, or until cabbage is tender. Add the sugar. Blend butter and flour and add to cabbage. Cook slowly, stirring constantly, until wine sauce is thickened and smooth.

SAUERKRAUT, SAUTERNE *(Serves 4)*

- 1 lb. sauerkraut, canned or bulk
- 3 tbsps. butter or margarine
- ½ cup Sauterne or Rhine Wine
- ½ cup water
- 2 tbsps. brown sugar

Combine sauerkraut and rest of ingredients in saucepan, and cook until liquid is reduced by half.

CALIFORNIA CARROTS *(Serves 4)*

- 2 tbsps. butter or margarine
- 4 cups shredded carrots
- 1 onion, minced
- ½ cup Sauterne or Rhine Wine

Melt margarine or butter in heavy saucepan, add shredded carrots and onion. Salt and pepper to taste, lightly. Add wine, cover, and cook gently on top of stove for 10 to 15 minutes, or until tender. If desired, this combination may be baked in a casserole in a moderate oven (350 degrees F.) for 25 to 30 minutes.

MUSHROOMS IN SHERRY *(Serves 6)*

- 1 lb. mushrooms
- ¼ cup butter or margarine
- ½ cup Sherry
- Salt and pepper
- 1 cup beef broth or
- 1 beef cube dissolved in 1 cup boiling water

Sauté the mushrooms in butter or margarine for 3 minutes. Add Sherry, beef broth, salt and pepper to taste, and simmer until mushrooms are tender—about 5 minutes.

STUFFED GREEN PEPPERS (*Serves 4*)

- 4 green peppers
- 4 small green onions
- 2 tbsps. butter or margarine
- 2 cups baked beans or
- 2 cups corned-beef hash
- ½ cup Claret or Burgundy

Wash peppers and cut in half lengthwise. Remove seeds. Plunge in boiling water. Parboil for 5 to 10 minutes. Remove to baking dish. Brown onions in butter or margarine. Add beans (or corned-beef hash) and wine and simmer slowly until most of the wine is absorbed. Fill mixture into peppers. Bake in a moderate oven (350 degrees F.) for 20 minutes.

MACARONI STUFFED PEPPERS, RED WINE (*Serves 6*)

- 6 green peppers
- 2 cups macaroni, cooked
- 1 cup cheese, diced
- 1 cup fresh tomatoes, diced
- ½ cup bread crumbs
- 1 onion, minced
- 1 tsp. salt
- ½ tsp. sugar
- ½ cup Claret or Burgundy

Cut a slice from the top of each green pepper. Remove seeds. Drop into boiling salted water and boil 5 minutes. Drain. Place in baking pan. Fill with mixture of remaining ingredients. Pour ½ inch of boiling water around the peppers. Bake for 30 minutes in a moderate oven (350 degrees F.).

SPLIT-PEA TIMBALES, SAUTERNE (*Serves 6*)

2 cups puréed green split peas
4 eggs, beaten
½ cup Sauterne or Rhine Wine
1½ tsps. salt
Pepper, cayenne
Grated onion

Add beaten eggs to puréed peas. Add wine, salt, pepper, cayenne, and a bit of grated onion. Pour into greased custard cups set in a pan of boiling water ½ inch deep. Bake at 350 degrees F. until firm—30 to 40 minutes. Serve with wine sauce as given below.

Sauterne Sauce for Timbales

3 tbsps. butter or margarine
3 tbsps. flour
1 cup water
2 bouillon cubes
2 tsps. paprika
¾ cup Sauterne or Rhine Wine

Heat butter or margarine with flour and stir in water. Add bouillon cubes, paprika, and simmer for 5 minutes. Add wine, and serve over split-pea timbales.

SPINACH SAUTERNE (*Serves 4*)

2 cups spinach, fresh cooked or canned, chopped
2 tsps. butter or margarine
¼ cup Sauterne or Rhine Wine
2 tsps. lemon juice
1 tsp. Worcestershire sauce

To drained chopped spinach add other ingredients. Heat. Add salt and pepper to taste. Serve at once.

SHERRIED SQUASH (*Serves 6*)

6 acorn squash
3 tbsps. butter or margarine
2 tbsps. brown sugar
1½ tsps. salt
½ tsp. mace
½ tsp. cinnamon
½ cup Sherry
12 pork sausages

Cut the squash in half and bake until done. Remove the pulp from the shells. Save six half shells. Mash pulp thoroughly. There should be about 2½ cups mashed squash. Add butter or margarine, sugar, salt, mace, and cinnamon. Add the wine gradually, cooking and stirring all the while. When all the wine is added, cook until squash is the consistency of mashed potatoes. Fill into the six squash half shells. Fry the sausages until almost done. Place two sausages on each serving of squash. Bake in a hot oven (450 degrees F.) for about 20 minutes.

STUFFED CROOKNECK SQUASH, RHINE WINE (*Serves 4*)

1 large crookneck squash
Butter
Rhine Wine or Sauterne
Brown sugar
Salt and pepper

Cut squash lengthwise and remove a 1-inch wedge from the entire length of the squash. Remove seeds and scoop out the pulp. Boil the pulp for 15 minutes. Drain well. Mash, and measure. (A large squash will yield approximately 2 cups of pulp.) To each cup of pulp add 2 tablespoons of wine, 2 tablespoons of melted butter, 1 teaspoon brown sugar, and salt and pepper to taste. Simmer slowly until enough of the liquid has cooked down to make squash proper consistency for refilling into shell. Refill squash shell, brush with melted butter, and brown quickly under the broiler.

STUFFED TOMATOES (*Serves 4*)

- 4 tomatoes
- 1 cup half-inch bread cubes
- 6 tbsps. butter or margarine
- 3 small green onions, chopped
- 2 frankfurters, sliced thin
- ½ cup Claret or Burgundy

Remove slice from top of each tomato. Scoop out pulp and juice into saucepan. Arrange tomatoes in baking dish. Brown the bread cubes in 4 tablespoons of the butter or margarine. Remove bread croutons from frying pan. Brown onions and frankfurters in remaining 2 tablespoons butter or margarine. Add the wine and the tomato pulp and simmer slowly for 10 minutes. Add the croutons. Fill mixture into tomato cups. Bake in a moderate oven (350 degrees F.) for 20 minutes.

BAKED STUFFED SWEET POTATOES (*Serves 6*)

- 6 medium-sized sweet potatoes
- ¾ cup Port
- Butter
- 1 egg
- 1 tsp. salt

Bake sweet potatoes until tender. Slice in halves, lengthwise, and scoop out the pulp. Mash well. Add 2 tablespoons butter, egg, wine, and salt. Whip until fluffy. Pile into shells, brush with butter, and bake in hot oven (450 degrees F.) for 8 minutes, until slightly browned.

GLAZED SWEET POTATOES (*Serves 6*)

6 medium-sized sweet potatoes	½ cup brown sugar
¼ cup butter or margarine	1 tsp. salt
	½ cup Sherry

Boil sweet potatoes until just tender. Remove jackets and split in half lengthwise. Grease baking pan with butter or margarine and spread with ¼ cup brown sugar. Sprinkle with salt and dot with butter or margarine. Arrange sweet potatoes in pan and pour on Sherry. Cover with remaining brown sugar and butter. Bake in a moderately hot oven (350 degrees F.) for half an hour, basting several times and turning once.

OMELET WITH MUSHROOMS IN RHINE WINE (*Serves 6*)

¼ cup butter or margarine	½ lb. fresh mushrooms, sliced
Juice of one lemon	6 eggs, beaten separately
Salt and pepper	6 tbsps. milk
½ cup Rhine Wine or Sauterne	

Heat 2 tablespoons of the butter or margarine in a skillet. Add the lemon juice, ½ teaspoon salt, dash of pepper, and the wine. Simmer mushrooms in this mixture until cooked.

Prepare omelet as follows: Add milk, ½ teaspoon salt, and dash of pepper to the egg yolks which have been beaten until light. Fold into stiffly beaten egg whites. Melt remaining 2 tablespoons butter or margarine in skillet, and heat well. Pour omelet mixture into hot skillet, and cook over low heat for 3 to 5 minutes. Then place omelet in a moderate oven (350 degrees F.), and bake for approximately 15 minutes. The omelet is done when it springs back when indented with the fingertip. Crease omelet through the center and place half the mushrooms on one side of the omelet, folding the other half of omelet over mushrooms. Serve on hot platter topped with remaining mushrooms.

SHERRIED EGGS ON TOAST (*Serves 6*)

6 eggs, hard-cooked
2 tbsps. butter or margarine
2 tbsps. green pepper, chopped
2 tbsps. flour
¾ cup milk
¼ cup Sherry
6 slices toast, buttered
½ tsp. salt
¼ tsp. pepper
½ tsp. Worcestershire sauce
1 tsp. sugar
¼ cup chili sauce (optional)

Melt the butter or margarine, add the green pepper, and cook 3 minutes. Shake flour and milk in a covered container until the mixture is smooth. Add to the butter and green pepper and cook, stirring constantly, until thickened and smooth. Add the Sherry, salt, pepper, Worcestershire sauce, and sugar. Add chili sauce if desired.

Slice the eggs and arrange one sliced egg on each slice of toast.

Pour sauce over the eggs on toast. Serve hot.

SHERRIED FRENCH TOAST (*Serves 2 to 3*)

2 eggs, beaten slightly
¼ tsp. salt
½ cup Sherry
5 or 6 slices bread (stale bread is best)
Oil or bacon fryings

Blend eggs, salt, and Sherry in a shallow dish. Dip bread slices quickly into mixture, coating both sides, and brown slowly in hot fat in a heavy skillet. Serve hot, sprinkled with sugar.

SHERRY CHEESE CANAPÉS

1 small pkg. Roquefort-type cheese
1 3-oz. pkg. cream cheese
Sherry
Cayenne

Combine the two cheeses, mashing with a fork. Blend to a paste with Sherry. Add a dash of cayenne. Spread on crisp crackers, or use to stuff celery.

CHEESE FONDUE (*Serves 3 to 4*)

2 tbsps. butter or margarine
3 tbsps. chives, chopped
1½ tbsps. flour
½ pound cheese, grated
1 cup Sauterne or Rhine Wine
Salt, pepper, nutmeg
2 egg yolks

Melt the butter. Add the chives and cook one minute. Add the wine. Heat to boiling. Dredge cheese in flour. Add slowly to hot wine. Stir until cheese is melted. Beat egg yolks. Pour small amount of hot cheese mixture over egg yolks. Add to cheese. Serve with bread or toast strips. Season to taste with salt, pepper, and nutmeg.

CHEESE RABBIT WITH SHERRY (*Serves 4 to 6*)

1 lb. American cheese
⅓ cup cream or evaporated milk
⅓ cup Sherry
½ tsp. Worcestershire sauce
1 tsp. mustard
Toast or crackers

Cut the cheese in cubes. Heat in top of double boiler or chafing dish until one fourth of the cheese is melted. Add the cream or evaporated milk. Stir over hot water until most of the cheese is melted, then add the Sherry slowly, stirring constantly, until cheese is melted and smooth. Add Worcestershire sauce and mustard. Serve hot on crackers or toast.

BAKED CHEESE SAVORY (*Serves 4*)

- 7 slices bread cut in 2-inch squares
- ½ lb. American cheese, sliced
- 3 eggs, beaten
- ½ tsp. paprika
- ½ tsp. salt
- ¼ tsp. dry mustard
- 2¼ cups milk
- ¼ cup Sherry

In a greased shallow baking dish arrange alternate layers of bread and sliced cheese. Beat eggs with paprika, salt, and mustard. Add milk and Sherry; pour over bread and cheese. Bake slowly at 325 degrees F. for 1 hour.

CHAPTER 8

FISH AND FISH SAUCES

Wine at the table promotes appetite, digestion, and well-being. Saucelike, it accents the flavors of foods.

ENCYCLOPAEDIA BRITANNICA

The white table wines, such as Sauterne and Rhine Wine, are generally chosen to accompany fish and shellfish because the light, piquant flavors of these wines complement the delicate flavors of most fish. In the following recipes which call for white table wine you will see we have suggested Sauterne or Rhine Wine. Each of these wines has its own individual flavor, and either will add delightful fragrance and zest to your foods. Any of the other white table wines may also be used in these recipes with equal success.

Sherry is another favorite wine in the preparation of fish dishes and may be added to the sauce or to a sea food cocktail, or used to marinate shrimp, flaked lobster, or crab for creamed or scalloped dishes.

BROILED FISH STEAKS (*Serves 4 to 6*)

2 lbs. halibut, salmon, or other fish steaks cut 1 inch thick
½ cup butter, margarine, or cooking oil
½ cup Sauterne or Rhine Wine, warm
Salt and pepper

Preheat broiler at 550 degrees F. for 10 minutes. Baste fish with mixture of melted butter, margarine, or cooking oil, and wine. Arrange pan with fish so that fish will be 2 inches from the source of heat. Broil for 2 minutes. Baste again. Broil for 2 to 3 minutes longer. Season with salt and pepper. Turn steaks. Baste with wine mixture. Return to broiler and broil for 2 minutes. Baste, and continue broiling until fish begins to flake and separate from the bone. Season with salt and pepper. Serve immediately.

BOUILLABAISSE (FISH STEW) *(Serves 4 to 6)*

2 lbs. fish
2 tbsps. lemon rind, grated
2 tbsps. parsley, minced
1 onion, chopped
1 small carrot, sliced
1 bay leaf
2 tomatoes, chopped
1 cup Sauterne or Rhine Wine
Salt and pepper
6 tbsps. butter or margarine
1 cup cooked shrimp, fresh or canned
2 tbsps. flour

The 2 pounds of fish should include at least two varieties of fish, one hard- and one soft-fleshed variety. Use head and tails for making a bouillon—cook in a quart of boiling water for ½ hour. Strain, and use as stock for cooking fish.

Skin the fish and remove the bones. Brown fish and onion in 4 tbsps. butter or margarine. Add carrot, lemon rind, parsley, tomatoes, bay leaf, and wine. Pour into soup kettle. Cover with the bouillon and cook rapidly for about 10 minutes, or until fish is tender and flaky. Add the shrimps and salt and pepper to taste. Blend flour in remaining butter or margarine and add to mixture. Cook until slightly thickened. Serve with toasted bread or with boiled rice.

CARP FILLETS, CLARET (*Serves 6*)

1 5-lb. carp
2 cups Claret or Burgundy
6 onions, sliced
½ tsp. ground mace
2 tbsps. parsley, chopped
2 bay leaves
1 tsp. salt
3 cups water
2 tbsps. butter or margarine
4 tbsps. flour
1 tsp. sugar
2 tbsps. orange juice
⅛ tsp. cayenne pepper

Skin carp and cut one large fillet from each side. Cut each into three pieces. Marinate in wine. Put onions, parsley, bay leaves, mace, salt, and water into saucepan. Cover, and simmer 15 minutes. Add fish and wine, and simmer, covered, for ½ hour. Melt butter or margarine in another saucepan. Blend in flour. Stir in 2 cups fish liquor. Bring to a boil, stirring constantly, until sauce thickens. Add sugar, orange juice, and cayenne pepper. Drain fillets and place on platter with lemon and parsley garnish. Serve at once with wine sauce.

BAKED FISH FILLETS, SANDWICH STYLE (*Serves 4*)

3 cups bread crumbs
¾ cup celery, chopped
3 tbsps. parsley, minced
¼ cup butter or margarine, melted
½ cup Sherry
1 egg, beaten
Salt, pepper, thyme to taste
8 small fillets of sole or flounder or thin slices halibut or salmon

Combine bread crumbs, celery, parsley, butter or margarine, Sherry, and beaten egg. Add salt, pepper, and thyme to taste. Salt and pepper fish fillets or slices and put together in pairs, sandwich style, with stuffing. Place on greased pan and bake, uncovered, in hot oven (400 degrees F.) for 30 to 40 minutes, or until done. Baste occasionally with Sherry and melted butter or margarine.

OVEN-FRIED FISH, WHITE WINE-AND-ALMOND SAUCE (*Serves 4*)

- 2 lbs. small fish, or fish fillets
- 1 cup Sauterne or Rhine Wine
- 2 tsps. salt
- Dry bread crumbs
- ½ cup butter or margarine
- ½ cup blanched almonds, halved
- 2 tbsps. lemon juice

Clean small brook fish, leaving on heads and tails if desired. Wash well under running water. Wipe dry. Dip in wine. (Reserve remaining wine for basting and for use in sauce.) Sprinkle with salt. Roll in dry crumbs. Place on greased shallow baking dish. Melt ¼ cup of butter or margarine and sprinkle over the fish. Bake in a very hot oven (500–550 degrees F.) for about 10 minutes until crumbs are crisp and brown. Remove from oven. Baste fish with about ¼ cup of the wine used for dipping fish. Return to oven for 3 to 5 minutes. Serve with Wine-and-Almond Sauce.

White Wine-and-Almond Sauce

Melt remaining butter or margarine in frying pan. Add the halved almonds and sauté until delicately browned. Add remaining wine and lemon juice. Bring to a full boil. Serve with fish. Garnish platter with lemon wedges and bunches of fresh water cress. Serve with hot, crisp potato chips.

PLANKED FISH, SAUTERNE (*Serves 8 to 10*)

4 to 5 lbs. white fish, trout, or any fish suitable for stuffing and baking
Salt and pepper
¼ cup butter or margarine, melted
4 slices bacon, chopped
2 tbsps. onion, minced
¼ cup celery, chopped fine
2 tbsps. green pepper, chopped
2 tbsps. parsley, chopped
¾ cup bread crumbs
2 cups Sauterne or Rhine Wine

Have fish cleaned without removing head and tail. Wash and dry inside and out. Rub inside and outside with salt and pepper and brush with 2 tablespoons melted butter or margarine. Broil the bacon in a skillet and when it begins to melt, add the onion, celery, green pepper, and parsley. Add remaining 2 tablespoons butter or margarine and the bread crumbs. Place filling in the fish and close with needle and stout thread. Bake on an oiled plank at temperature about 400 degrees F. Allow about 10 minutes per pound. Baste at intervals with wine. Baste with heated wine immediately before serving.

MUSHROOM SAUCE FOR FISH, SAUTERNE
(*Makes one cup sauce*)

½ lb. mushrooms, sliced
¼ cup butter or margarine
½ tsp. salt
Dash pepper
½ cup Sauterne or Rhine Wine
1 bouillon cube
½ cup boiling water
1 tbsp. flour
2 tbsps. lemon juice
½ tsp. mustard
¼ tsp. Worcestershire sauce

Sauté mushrooms lightly in 2 tablespoons butter or margarine. Add salt, pepper, and wine. Cook for 5 minutes. Disolve bouillon cube in boiling water and add to mushroom mixture. Blend flour with remaining 2 tablespoons butter or margarine and add to hot liquid. Cook until thickened. Season with lemon juice. The measure of mustard and Worcestershire sauce is optional. Serve sauce with broiled fish.

FILLET OF SOLE, MARGUERY (*Serves 4*)

4 fillets of sole
½ cup Sauterne or Rhine Wine
1 tbsp. lemon juice
¼ cup butter or margarine
Salt, pepper, and paprika
½ lemon, sliced
1 tbsp. flour
3 tbsps. cream
1 egg yolk, slightly beaten
½ tsp. sugar

Arrange fillets in buttered baking dish. Pour on the wine, lemon juice, and 3 tablespoons of the melted butter or margarine. Sprinkle with salt, pepper, and paprika. Top with lemon slices. Bake in a hot oven (450 degrees F.) for 15 to 20 minutes, or until fish begins to flake. Transfer fish to hot platter and keep hot.

Prepare sauce as follows: Melt remaining 1 tablespoon butter or margarine. Blend in the flour. Add hot wine mixture in which fish was baked. Cook, stirring constantly, until thickened and smooth. Add cream to beaten egg yolk. Pour small amount of hot sauce into egg-yolk mixture. Add to remaining hot sauce. Cook for 1 minute over very low flame, or over hot water. Add sugar. Sprinkle chopped parsley over fish fillets. Serve topped with sauce.

BOILED SALMON IN COURT BOUILLON
(*Serves 4*)

1 2-lb. slice salmon or other firm-fleshed fish
2 carrots, sliced
2 slices onion
¼ cup celery, chopped
¼ cup butter or margarine
1½ qts. water
1 tbsp. salt
2 whole cloves
6 peppercorns
1 bay leaf
½ cup vinegar
2 cups Sauterne or Rhine Wine

To prepare Court Bouillon: Brown the carrots, onion, and celery in the butter or margarine. Bring the water to boiling point, add the vegetables, salt, spices, and vinegar. Simmer for 10 minutes. Add the wine.

Sew or wrap the salmon in cheesecloth (or arrange on cooking rack) and lower into boiling broth. Cover and simmer for 20 to 30 minutes, or until fish begins to flake. Retain Court Bouillon for use in Sauce Piquante below.

Sauce Piquante

2 egg yolks
2 tbsps. butter or margarine
½ cup Court Bouillon
¼ cup Sauterne or Rhine Wine
2 tbsps. lemon juice
¼ cup pickles, chopped
1 tsp. sugar

Beat egg yolks until very light. Add to the butter or margarine, stirring until creamy and smooth. Heat Court Bouillon and wine and add to creamed egg and butter mixture gradually. Cook over hot water until thickened, stirring constantly. Add the lemon juice and chopped pickles. Add sugar if desired.

BAKED HALIBUT, WHITE WINE (*Serves 6*)

2 lbs. sliced halibut
1 cup Sauterne or Rhine Wine
1 tbsp. salt
Pepper
1½ cups fine cracker crumbs
¼ cup butter or margarine
3 tbsps. flour
¾ cup light cream
1 tsp. chives, minced
1 tsp. parsley, minced
1 tsp. nutmeg
1 tbsp. lemon juice

Set oven temperature at 500 degrees F. Dip halibut in wine to which 1 teaspoon salt has been added. Then dip in fine crumbs and sprinkle with remaining salt and pepper as desired. Heat cooking fat in the oven in a large flat baking pan. Place crumbed halibut in pan and baste with hot fat. Bake uncovered for 10 minutes, or until the crumbs are browned and fish begins to flake.

Melt the butter in a saucepan and blend in the flour. Add ½ cup of the wine used for dipping fish and cook, stirring constantly, until the mixture boils and thickens. Add the cream, and stir until smooth. Stir in chives, parsley, nutmeg, lemon juice, and salt to taste. Pour sauce over hot fish on a platter garnished with parsley and lemon wedges.

BAKED SMELTS, SAUTERNE (*Serves 6*)

2 pounds smelts
1 cup celery, chopped
¼ cup parsley, minced
½ cup Sauterne or Rhine Wine
Salt and pepper
½ cup bread crumbs
1 cup mushrooms, sliced
6 tbsps. butter or margarine

Clean and dry the smelts. Remove the heads, if desired. Arrange a layer of chopped celery and parsley in the bottom of a shallow baking dish. Place smelts on the vegetables. Pour wine over smelts. Sprinkle with salt and pepper and bread crumbs. Arrange mushrooms on top. Dot with butter or margarine. Bake in a very hot oven (500 degrees F.) for about 10 minutes. Baste the smelts once with wine from bottom of pan. Serve in baking dish.

FILLET OF SOLE, SAUTERNE (*Serves 4*)

- 8 small fillets of sole or flounder
- 1 tbsp. butter or margarine
- 1 tsp. onion, chopped
- 1 tsp. parsley, chopped
- 2 or 3 mushrooms, chopped fine
- 1 stalk celery, chopped
- 1 bay leaf
- 1 cup Sauterne or Rhine Wine
- ½ cup water
- 1 bouillon cube

Salt and pepper fillets. Melt the butter or margarine in a large skillet and add other ingredients. Lay the fillets in the hot liquid and let simmer for 5 to 10 minutes, until barely tender. Remove carefully to oven-proof platter or shallow baking dish. Boil down the liquid in which fish was cooked until about ¾ cup remains. Add 2 tablespoons cream, more seasonings if needed. Strain the liquid over fish in the baking dish, sprinkle grated Parmesan cheese over all, and bake on the upper shelf of a hot oven (450 degrees F.) for about 10 minutes, or until the top is lightly browned.

MARYLAND CRAB CAKES (*Serves 4*)

1 lb. can crab meat, shredded
4 eggs
½ tsp. salt
¼ tsp. pepper
¼ cup Sherry
3 tbsps. celery, chopped
1 tbsp. parsley, chopped
2 tbsps. chives, chopped

Mix ingredients in order given. Drop by spoonfuls in hot butter or margarine in skillet. Brown on both sides. Serve immediately.

SHERRIED DEVILED CRAB (*Serves 6*)

2 cups crab meat, fresh cooked or canned
2 hard-cooked eggs, chopped
1 cup mayonnaise or medium white sauce
1 tsp. grated onion
1 tsp. parsley, chopped
2 tsps. lemon juice
½ tsp. Worcestershire sauce
½ tsp. prepared mustard
3 tbsps. Sherry
1 cup bread crumbs, buttered.

Combine crab meat, chopped eggs, mayonnaise or white sauce, and seasonings. Add Sherry and ½ cup bread crumbs. Fill six buttered crab or scallop shells or ramekins, sprinkle with remaining crumbs, and bake in a moderately hot oven (400 degrees F.) for about 15 to 20 minutes, or until crumbs are browned.

SHERRIED CRAB MEAT IN AVOCADO (*Serves 4*)

2 medium avocados
1 cup crab meat, cooked or canned
½ cup Sherry
1 tsp. lemon juice

Peel avocados and cut in half lengthwise. Remove stone. Marinate crab meat in Sherry for 20 minutes. Fill avocado with crab meat and Sherry, add a dash of lemon juice, and serve garnished with a slice of lemon and a bit of curly endive.

CRAB MEAT NEWBURG (*Serves 4*)

3 tbsps. butter
1 lb. or 1 large can crab meat
Salt
Paprika
½ cup Sherry
2 egg yolks
½ cup cream

Melt butter in large saucepan. Add the flaked crab meat. Season with salt and paprika, and sauté lightly for 4 or 5 minutes. Add Sherry, and let simmer for 5 minutes. Just before serving add the egg yolks beaten up in cream and cook, stirring gently, until thickened. Do not let the mixture boil. Serve on toast.

LOBSTER THERMIDOR (*Serves 4*)

2 small boiled lobsters
⅔ cup Sherry
4 tbsps. butter or margarine
1½ cups fresh mushrooms
2 tbsps. dry mustard
2 cups medium white sauce
Salt and pepper
½ cup fine cracker crumbs

Split boiled lobsters lengthwise and discard dark portion. Remove meat from body and claws, cut in pieces, and add Sherry. Melt butter or margarine in frying pan, add sliced mushrooms, and sauté for 3 minutes. Add mustard and white sauce, season to taste, and blend well. Add the Sherried lobster meat, mixing thoroughly. Place in lobster shells, cover with cracker crumbs, bake in hot oven (400 degrees F.) until browned.

OYSTER COCKTAIL (*Serves 4*)

24 small oysters, chilled
½ cup Sherry
Salt, pepper, and tabasco sauce to taste

Place oysters in cocktail glasses. Cover with seasoned Sherry, and serve with lemon wedges.

OYSTER STEW, WHITE WINE (*Serves 4*)

2 tbsps. butter or margarine
1 pint oysters
1 pint milk, scalded
1 cup Sauterne or Rhine Wine
1 cup cream

Melt butter or margarine. Add oysters and cook until edges begin to curl. Season with salt and pepper. Scald milk and oyster liquor. Add to oysters. Heat to boiling point. Remove from flame. Add wine gradually. Finally add the cream. Reheat, and serve very hot.

OYSTER CASSEROLE, SAUTERNE (*Serves 6*)

1 cup sliced mushrooms
6 to 8 small, whole mushrooms
4 tbsps. butter or margarine
1 cup fine cracker crumbs
1½ pint oysters
½ cup oyster liquor
½ cup rich milk
½ cup Sauterne or Rhine Wine
Paprika

Sauté all mushrooms in 2 tablespoons butter or margarine for 2 minutes. Line greased baking dish or individual casseroles with one-third of the crumbs. Add layer of sliced mushrooms and a layer of crumbs, then add oysters, remaining sliced mushrooms, and a final layer of crumbs. Scald oyster liquor and milk. Add wine and remaining 2 tablespoons butter or margarine, melted, and pour the mixture over top of casserole. Bake in moderately hot oven (375 degrees F.) for 25 minutes. Stand whole mushrooms upright in crumbs, sprinkle with paprika, and return to oven 2 or 3 minutes. Serve hot.

OYSTER AND MACARONI CASSEROLE
(*Serves 4*)

1 pint raw or canned oysters, drained
2 cups medium white sauce
3 tbsps. Sherry
2 cups cooked macaroni
Grated cheese

Heat oysters in well-seasoned white sauce. Add Sherry. Place a layer of macaroni in buttered casserole. Cover with creamed oysters. Top with remaining macaroni, and sprinkle with grated cheese. Bake in medium oven (350 degrees F.) for 15 minutes.

OYSTERS, CHARLOTTE (*Serves 6*)

1½ pints large oysters
1½ cups Sauterne or Rhine Wine
1 tbsp. lemon juice
3 tbsps. butter or margarine
3 tbsps. flour
½ cup rich milk
½ tsp. salt
Pepper
½ tsp. nutmeg
2 cups cooked crab meat or shrimp
¼ cup fine bread crumbs

Poach the oysters in the wine and lemon juice until the edges begin to curl. Melt 2 tablespoons butter or margarine, blend in the flour, and stir in the wine in which the oysters were poached. Stir constantly until the mixture boils and thickens. Stir in the milk, salt, pepper, and nutmeg. Combine 1 cup of the white sauce with the crab meat or shrimp which have been mashed or minced. Arrange crab meat or shrimp mixture in scallop shells or ramekins. Place 2 or 3 poached oysters on each and pour a spoonful of sauce over the oysters. Top with crumbs, dot with remaining butter or margarine, and brown quickly under the broiler. Serve very hot with wedges of lemon.

SHRIMP-GRAPEFRUIT COCKTAIL (*Serves 6*)

- 2 doz. cooked or canned shrimps
- 2 grapefruit, sectioned
- Lettuce
- 1 cup cocktail sauce
- ½ cup Sherry

Marinate shrimp and grapefruit sections in the Sherry for about 1 hour. Add ¼ cup of the Sherry in which the shrimp and grapefruit were marinated to the cocktail sauce. Arrange shrimp and grapefruit sections alternately on glass plates. Center each plate with a serving of cocktail sauce.

SHRIMP COCKTAIL, SHERRY (*Serves 6*)

- 2 cups cooked or canned shrimps
- ½ cup tomato catsup
- ¼ cup chili sauce
- ¼ cup lemon juice
- 1 tsp. horseradish
- 1 tsp. green pepper, chopped
- ½ cup Sherry
- Salt

Place shrimps in individual serving glasses. Mix remaining ingredients together and add to shrimps. Chill in refrigerator until ready to serve.

SHERRIED SHRIMPS CREOLE (*Serves 6*)

- 2 lbs. fresh shrimps or 4 cups cooked and cleaned
- ¼ cup butter or margarine
- 2 tbsps. onion, chopped fine
- 1 cup canned tomatoes or 2 large tomatoes cut in pieces
- 1 bay leaf
- ½ tsp. salt
- ½ tsp. thyme
- Dash cayenne
- 1 tsp. sugar
- 1 can condensed mushroom soup
- ⅓ cup Sherry
- 2 pimientos cut in strips

Wash shrimps in cold water. Drop into boiling salted water and cook for 15 to 20 minutes. Drain. Cover with cold water. Remove shells and legs. Clean by removing dark vein along back of each shrimp. Melt the butter or margarine. Cook onion in butter or margarine until it turns yellow. Add the tomatoes, bay leaf, salt, thyme, cayenne, and sugar. Dilute the mushroom soup with the Sherry, and add to tomato mixture. Finally add the shrimps and pimientos. Cook for 5 minutes. Serve with hot boiled rice.

SHRIMP NEWBURG (*Serves 4*)

- 2 cups cooked or canned shrimps
- 3 tbsps. margarine or cooking oil
- ¼ cup Sherry
- 1½ cups light cream or rich milk
- 3 egg yolks
- 2 tsps. flour
- Paprika
- Nutmeg
- Salt

Sauté shrimps lightly in margarine or cooking oil in top of chafing dish or over low heat. Add the Sherry and cook a few minutes longer. Add 1 cup light cream or rich milk and heat thoroughly. Beat egg yolks and flour into remaining ½ cup cream or milk. Pour small amount of hot mixture into the beaten eggs. Add eggs to hot mixture slowly. Cook over hot water in chafing dish or double boiler, stirring constantly, until thickened and smooth. Add dash of paprika, nutmeg, and salt to taste. Serve on hot toast points.

FISH COCKTAIL SAUCE (*Serves 8 to 10*)

⅔ cup catsup
⅓ cup Sherry
2 tbsps. vinegar
1 tbsp. horseradish
1 tbsp. green pepper, diced
1 tbsp. onion, minced
1 tsp. Worcestershire sauce
Few drops tabasco sauce
Salt and pepper to taste

Mix ingredients and chill. Serve over flaked fish, shrimps, or oysters, or serve in a dish for dipping whole shrimps. This recipe makes 1½ cups sauce.

SEA FOOD SCALLOP (*Serves 6*)

2 cups shrimp, fresh cooked or canned
2 cups flaked cooked crab meat
1 pound mushrooms
½ green pepper, diced
¼ cup butter or margarine
2 cups medium white sauce
½ cup Sherry
¼ cup pimiento, cut in strips

Sauté mushrooms and green pepper in the butter for 4 minutes. Add shrimp and crab meat and the white sauce to which the Sherry and the pimiento have been added. Pour into casserole, top with croutons, and bake in a hot oven (425 degrees F.) for about 10 minutes. Serve on toast.

CREAMED SEA FOOD AU GRATIN (*Serves 4*)

¼ cup cream
1 medium-sized can of tuna, salmon, shrimp, or crab
1 10½ oz. can condensed cream of mushroom soup
2 tbsps. Sherry
Grated cheese

Add cream and coarsely flaked sea food to soup, and heat gently over direct heat or in a double boiler. Add wine, and pour into shallow baking dish. Sprinkle top with buttered crumbs and grated cheese. Bake in moderately hot oven (400 degrees F.) for 15 minutes, until thoroughly hot and lightly browned.

SEA FOOD À LA KING (*Serves 4*)

2 tbsps. butter or margarine
1 green pepper, diced
2 tbsps. sliced pimiento
1 cup canned or cooked sliced mushrooms
1 tbsp. flour
½ tsp. salt
⅛ tsp. pepper
¼ tsp. paprika
1 cup light cream
1 cup cooked shrimp
1 cup cooked flaked fish
3 egg yolks
¼ cup Sherry
Toast

Melt butter or margarine in a chafing dish. Add the green pepper, pimiento, and mushrooms and cook, stirring, for 3 minutes, or until the pepper is soft. Stir in the flour, salt, pepper, and paprika. Gradually add the cream, stirring constantly. Add the shrimp and the flaked fish. Beat the egg yolks light, add the wine, and stir into the à la King mixture. Cook, stirring constantly, until mixture thickens. Serve on toast.

SEA FOOD NEWBURG (*Serves 4*)

1 small can tuna fish, flaked
1 small can shrimps
¼ cup butter or margarine
¼ cup Sherry
3 egg yolks, slightly beaten
¾ cup light cream
1 tbsp. lemon juice
½ tsp. salt
Pinch cayenne
Pinch nutmeg

Cook tuna and shrimps lightly in butter or margarine. Add wine, and cook 1 minute. Mix egg yolks with cream and cook, stirring constantly, until mixture thickens. Add to sea food and Sherry. Add lemon juice. salt, cayenne, and nutmeg. Serve on toast points.

NEWBURG SAUCE

2 tsps. flour
½ cup butter or margarine
¾ cup rich milk or cream
2 egg yolks
½ tsp. salt
Dash pepper
½ tsp. nutmeg
6 tbsps. Sherry

Heat butter or margarine and blend in flour. Add the milk, and cook slowly, stirring constantly, until thickened and smooth. Add the wine and beaten egg yolks. Heat just to boiling, but do not boil. Season with salt, pepper, and nutmeg. Lobster, shrimp, or crab meat may be combined with the sauce.

CHAPTER *9*

MEATS AND MEAT SAUCES

My manner of living is plain and I do not mean to be put out of it. A glass of wine and a bit of mutton are always ready and such as will be content to partake of that are always welcome. . . .

GEORGE WASHINGTON

In the cooking of meats with wine, a good general guide to follow is red table wines, such as Claret and Burgundy, with red meats; white table wines, such as Sauterne and Rhine Wine, with meats like pork and veal. Sherry blends harmoniously with either red or white meats, and for new flavor variety may be substituted for the red or white table wines. Brains and sweetbreads are usually best with a white table wine or Sherry. Tongue combines well with either red or white table wine, or Sherry.

There are three primary ways in which wine may be used to enrich the flavors of meat and meat dishes:

Wine may replace part of the water or other liquid in the meat recipe, or in the sauce or gravy with which the dish is to be served.

Wine may be used for basting, when broiling, roasting, or baking.

Wine may be used to marinate meats before cooking.

WINE MARINATING

Wine marinating serves a double purpose in the preparation of meats, for wine not only helps to improve the texture and tenderize tough, stringy meats, but it also adds delicious new flavor to otherwise tasteless cuts.

The dictionary says marinating means "to let stand." Wine marinating is as easy as that. Simply pour some of your table wine over the meat and let it stand for a few hours before cooking, turning the meat occasionally during the marinating period. If the meat is thin cut, even an hour's marinating will work wonders. For roasts or thicker cuts, allow the meat to marinate in the wine for several hours before cooking.

If you have any of the wine marinade left over, use it to baste the meat while it's roasting or broiling.

TOMATO BEEF STEW, BURGUNDY

(*Serves 6 to 8*)

2 lbs. beef stew meat, cut in 2-inch cubes
1½ cups Burgundy or Claret
Suet or cooking fat
1 clove garlic, minced
1 cup celery, diced
3 cloves
1 bay leaf
3 small potatoes, pared and cut in halves
1 lb. tomatoes, peeled and quartered, or 3 cups solid-pack canned tomatoes
2 tbsps. browned flour

Add wine to beef cubes and let stand for 2 or 3 hours. Drain. Brown meat in hot fat. Season, and add garlic, celery, cloves, and bay leaf. Add the wine in which the meat was marinated, and enough water to cover the meat (about 1 cup). Cover kettle, and simmer for 1 hour. Add vegetables. Continue simmering for 1 hour longer, or until tender. Five minutes before serving thicken with paste made of browned flour and a little water.

BEEF STEW, CLARET (*Serves 4*)

- 1 lb. chuck beef, cut in cubes
- ¼ cup flour
- 1½ tsps. salt
- ¼ tsp. pepper
- 1 cup cold water
- ½ cup Claret or Burgundy
- 4 onions
- 4 small potatoes
- 8 small carrots

Roll beef in flour to which salt and pepper have been added. Sauté in hot fat until browned on all sides. Add water and wine, and simmer very slowly for about 1 hour. Add onions, potatoes, and carrots and continue cooking for 25 to 30 minutes longer.

POT ROAST, RED WINE (*Serves 6*)

- 3 lbs. chuck or other beef
- 1 cup water
- 1 cup Claret or Burgundy
- 1 clove garlic
- ¼ cup flour
- 1 tsp. salt
- ¼ tsp. pepper
- 6 tbsps. cooking fat
- 6 small whole onions
- 6 carrots, cut in half lengthwise
- 6 potatoes

Wipe meat with damp cloth. Pour wine and water over meat. Add garlic clove. Allow to stand in refrigerator for about 6 hours, or overnight. Remove meat from marinade. Discard garlic, keep wine-and-water marinade.

Rub meat on all sides with mixture of flour, salt, and pepper. Sear in cooking fat. Add half the marinade. Cover tightly, and allow to simmer slowly over low heat for about 2½ hours. More water may be added from time to time to keep about 1 cup of liquid in pan at all times. Then add onions, carrots, potatoes, and remaining half of wine marinade. Cook for ½ hour. Remove meat and vegetables to hot platter. Season, and thicken gravy as desired.

RIB ROAST, BURGUNDY (*Serves 4 to 6*)

2 or 3 ribs of beef
Salt, pepper, flour
2 cups Burgundy or Claret

Wipe roast with damp cloth and place on open roasting pan. Rub with salt, pepper, and flour. Place in hot oven (500 degrees F.), and sear for 20 minutes. Then reduce heat to 300 degrees F. and continue roasting, allowing 18 to 20 minutes per pound for rare roast, 22 to 25 minutes per pound for medium roast, and about 30 minutes per pound for well-done roast. Baste frequently with wine.

BEEF CASSEROLE, BURGUNDY (*Serves 4*)

1 lb. beef (round steak, chuck, or rump)
3 tbsps. flour
1 tsp. salt
¼ tsp. pepper
Suet or cooking fat
2 onions, sliced
1 cup Burgundy or Claret
1 cup carrots, sliced
1½ cups mashed potatoes
1 egg yolk, beaten

Cut beef into ½-inch cubes. Mix flour, salt, and pepper. Dredge beef cubes in flour mixture. Fry out suet or melt cooking fat. Brown onions lightly. Remove to casserole. Brown beef cubes in fat. Add wine, and simmer slowly for about ½ hour, or until meat is tender. Add water as needed when gravy becomes too thick. Add the browned onions and the carrots. Turn into shallow casserole. Bake in a moderate oven (350 degrees F.) for about 30 minutes. Garnish the top of the casserole with mashed potatoes that have been forced through a pastry gun. Drip beaten egg yolk over mashed potatoes. Brown in hot oven (450 degrees F.).

BEEF JULIENNE (*Serves 6*)

1 tbsp. butter or margarine
1 medium onion, chopped
1 tbsp. flour
1 cup bouillon, canned or made with cubes
Salt and pepper
Worcestershire sauce
½ cup Claret or Burgundy
Thick slices cold, cooked roast beef

Melt butter or margarine in frying pan and fry onion until golden brown. Blend in flour, mix well, then add bouillon and cook, stirring until blended. Season to taste. Add wine, and continue stirring. Put in sliced roast beef and let heat slowly.

BEEFSTEAK PIE, RED WINE (*Serves 4*)

1½ lbs. round steak
Flour
1 tsp. salt
⅛ tsp. pepper
Water
¾ cup Claret or Burgundy
Plain pastry for topping pies
Beef suet from steak and cooking fat as needed to brown steak

Trim suet from steak and fry out the suet in skillet. Cut steak into ¾-inch cubes. Dredge in ¼ cup flour to which the salt and pepper have been added. Add cooking fat to fried-out suet if necessary for browning onions and steak. Brown onions and steak in hot fat. Remove onions to plate to be added to meat after meat has cooked 20 minutes. Add ½ cup water and ¼ cup of the wine to the steak, and simmer in a covered skillet. After 20 minutes add the onions. Add remaining wine and water as needed to keep meat and onions simmering in gravy. Cook for 30 minutes.

Remove meat and onions to baking dishes. If gravy is too thin, thicken with flour blended with butter or margarine. (About 1 tablespoon each should be right.) Cook, stirring constantly, until thickened and smooth. Pour over meat and onions in casseroles. Top with pastry. Bake in a hot oven (400 degrees F.) for 15 to 20 minutes until pastry is browned.

BEEF AND KIDNEY PIE (*Serves 6*)

- 1¾ lbs. round steak, cut in cubes
- 3 lamb kidneys
- 1 cup potato balls
- ½ cup carrot balls
- 1 medium onion, sliced
- 1½ cups Claret or Burgundy
- 1 tsp. salt
- ⅛ tsp. pepper
- 2 tbsps. butter or margarine
- 2 tbsps. flour
- Plain pastry

Boil potato balls and carrot balls separately for 15 minutes. Split the kidneys in half lengthwise and remove the tubes. Soak in cold water (slightly salted) for ½ hour. Brown the onion in bacon drippings. Add the beef, and brown on all sides. Add 1 cup water and simmer, covered, over low heat for ¾ hour.

Brown the kidneys in 1 tablespoon butter or margarine, turning occasionally. Simmer 10 minutes. Add to beef cubes. Add wine to meat, and heat. Season with salt and papper. Remove beef and kidneys from wine gravy. Blend flour with remaining butter or margarine, and add to hot wine gravy. Cook until slightly thickened. Put meat and vegetables in buttered casserole. Pour on hot gravy. Top with pastry crust, pricking the crust in several places to allow steam to escape. Bake in hot oven (400 degrees F.) for about 20 minutes until browned.

BROILED STEAK, BURGUNDY SAUCE
(*Serves 4 to 5*)

- 1 porterhouse or sirloin steak, 2 to 4 lbs. cut thick
- 2 tbsps. minced onion
- 3 tbsps. butter or margarine
- ¼ cup water
- ¾ cup Burgundy or Claret
- Salt and pepper
- 1 tbsp. flour

Cook the onion in the butter or margarine for 3 minutes. Add the flour. Stir in the water and the wine. Heat to boiling, and simmer for 10 minutes. Season to taste with salt and pepper. (If desired, add ½ teaspoon Worcestershire sauce and 1 teaspoon sugar.) Skim fat from steak drippings and add juices to sauce. Pour over and around broiled steak on hot platter or serve from gravy boat.

SWISS STEAK, RED WINE (*Serves 8*)

- 3 lbs. round steak, about 1½″ thick
- ⅓ cup flour
- 1½ tsps. salt
- ¼ tsp. pepper
- ¼ cup cooking fat
- 3 medium onions
- 1 green pepper, sliced
- 1 cup celery, cut in pieces
- 1½ cups Claret or Burgundy
- 1 cup tomato juice

Dredge the steak in flour to which salt and pepper have been added. Pound with meat pounder or the edge of a saucer. Brown on all sides in hot cooking fat. Add onions, green pepper, celery, and ¾ cup wine. Cover, and bake in a moderate oven (350 degrees F.) for ½ hour. Then add remaining wine and the tomato juice, and continue baking, covered, for approximately 1 hour longer.

CORNED BEEF WITH SHERRY GLAZE
(*Serves 12 to 15*)

6 to 7 lbs. corned beef
¾ cup Sherry
½ cup brown sugar
10 whole cloves

Wash corned beef under running water to remove brine. Cover with cold water and bring to a boil. Drain, and replace water. Simmer slowly in a covered kettle for about 4½ hours, or until meat is tender, adding more water as necessary.

Drain beef and place on baking rack. Pour Sherry over surface of beef and sprinkle brown sugar over all. Stick with cloves. Bake in a moderate oven (350 degrees F.) for about ½ hour.

SPICED BEEF IN RED WINE (*Serves 6 to 8*)

3 to 4 lbs. pot roast
2 cups water
½ cup vinegar
4 tsps. salt
1 tsp. peppercorns
½ tsp. mace
Carrots
2 onions, sliced
½ cup brown sugar
2 tsps. mixed-pickle spices
1½ cups Claret or Burgundy
Flour to thicken gravy

Combine water, vinegar, peppercorns, mace, sliced onions, brown sugar, and pickle spices. Bring to boiling point. Add the wine, and pour over the roast. Store in refrigerator overnight.

Rub roast with salt, and brown on all sides. Pour half the sauce over roast and simmer, covered, for about two hours. Add remaining spice sauce and the carrots, and simmer for 1 hour longer. Measure liquid in bottom of pan. Thicken with flour, allowing 2 tablespoons flour for each cup of liquid. Serve with noodles or dumplings.

WINE HAMBURGERS (*Serves 4 to 6*)

- 1½ cups dry bread crumbs or 1 cup bran
- 1 medium onion, minced
- ¾ cup Claret or Burgundy
- 1 egg, beaten
- 1 lb. beef, ground
- 1½ tsps. salt
- ¼ tsp. pepper

Pour wine over bread crumbs or bran. Add the minced onion. When bread is soft, add the beaten egg, ground beef, salt, and pepper. Mix well. Form into eight patties. Brown in hot fat in skillet.

STUFFED ROLL OF BEEF, RED WINE (*Serves 6*)

- 1 slice round steak, cut ¼″ thick (about 2 lbs.)
- Flour
- 1 cup sausage meat
- 2 cups bread crumbs
- 2 eggs
- 2 tbsps. parsley, minced
- 2 tbsps. green pepper, chopped
- 2 tbsps. onion, minced
- ¼ cup butter or margarine
- Salt, pepper
- Milk
- 2 cups cooked or canned tomatoes
- 1½ cups Claret or Burgundy

Make stuffing by combining sausage meat, bread crumbs, parsley, and eggs. Brown green pepper and onion in the butter or margarine and add to mixture. Add salt and pepper to taste, and enough milk to moisten. Arrange dressing along center of round steak. Bring edges of steak around dressing and sew or close with skewers. Dredge steak in flour, and brown on all sides. Place in casserole. Cover with tomatoes and wine. Bake in a moderate oven (350 degrees F.) for 1 hour. Serve on a hot platter garnished with fresh green vegetables. Use juices as gravy. Thicken gravy with flour if desired.

BURGUNDY MEAT LOAF *(Serves 4 to 5)*

- 1 lb. ground beef
- ¾ cup rolled oats
- ½ cup Burgundy or Claret
- 3 tbsp. onion, chopped
- 1¼ tsps. salt
- ¼ tsp. pepper
- ⅛ tsp. poultry seasoning
- 1 egg, beaten
- 2 tbsps. melted meat fryings

Combine beef, rolled oats, and wine. Add onion, salt, pepper, poultry seasoning, and mix. Add beaten egg and melted meat fryings. Pack into small, greased loaf pan, and bake in moderate oven (350 degrees F.) for 1 hour, or until done.

CALIFORNIA HASH, BURGUNDY *(Serves 6)*

- 2 cups cooked beef, chopped
- 1 cup Burgundy or Claret
- 1 cup onions, chopped
- 3 tbsps. butter
- 1 tbsp. flour
- 2 tsps. prepared mustard
- Salt, pepper

Cook the onions in the butter until browned. Then add the beef, and simmer for 5 minutes. Stir in the flour.

Heat wine in saucepan, then add to other ingredients. Add mustard, salt, and pepper. Serve on platter surrounded by cooked whole carrots and Lima beans.

MEAT BALLS AND SPAGHETTI, CLARET

(*Serves 6*)

Meat Balls

1 lb. beef, ground
1 egg
1 tsp. salt
⅛ tsp. sage leaves, crushed
⅛ tsp. pepper
1 small onion, chopped
½ cup bread crumbs
⅓ cup Claret or Burgundy
Flour
Cooking fat

Spaghetti and Sauce

¼ cup cooking oil or bacon fat
½ clove garlic, chopped
1 onion, sliced
1 tbsp. parsley, chopped
2⅓ cups tomato purée
½ tsp. salt
⅛ tsp. pepper
Dash cayenne
1 bay leaf
1 cup Claret or Burgundy
1 8-oz. pkg. spaghetti

Prepare meat balls as follows: Mix beef, egg, salt, pepper, sage, onion, bread crumbs, and wine. Form into 12 meat balls. Roll in flour, and sauté in fat until brown. Add to spaghetti, and simmer 15 minutes. Serve with grated Parmesan-style cheese.

Prepare spaghetti and sauce as follows: Cook garlic, onion, and parsley in cooking oil or bacon fat for 10 minutes. Add tomato purée, salt, pepper, cayenne, bay leaf, and wine. Simmer, stirring frequently, for 1 hour. Cook spaghetti in a large kettle, using about 3 quarts of boiling water and 3 teaspoons salt. Cook for 9 to 12 minutes. Wash with cold water. Add to sauce.

SWEDISH MEAT BALLS, CLARET SAUCE
(*Serves 5 to 6*)

1 lb. beef, ground twice if possible
1 cup fine, dry bread crumbs
1 tsp. cornstarch
1 tsp. salt
¼ tsp. pepper
Dash allspice or mace
1 egg, beaten
1 cup top milk
1 small onion, minced
Fat or oil for sautéing
3 tbsps. flour
2 cups water
⅔ cup Claret or Burgundy
Salt, pepper

Add bread crumbs, cornstarch, salt, pepper, allspice or mace, beaten egg, and top milk to the ground meat. Sauté onion lightly in fat or oil. Mix with ground meat mixture. Blend ingredients thoroughly. Shape into 1-inch balls, 40 or 42 in all. Brown lightly in a little oil or fat. Take up balls. Make gravy by stirring the flour into fat in pan and adding the water and the wine. Add salt and pepper to gravy to taste. Return meat balls to pan, and simmer for 20 minutes.

SPAGHETTI MEAT CASSEROLE
(*Serves 4 to 5*)

1 medium onion, minced
1 clove garlic, minced
½ green pepper, minced
¼ cup meat fryings
½ lb. ground beef
2½ cups diced fresh or canned tomatoes
1 tsp. sugar
Salt and pepper
½ cup Claret or Burgundy
3 cups cooked spaghetti
¼ lb. cheese, grated

Fry minced onion, garlic, and green pepper in meat fryings until limp but not browned. Add ground meat and cook, stirring, until seared. Add tomatoes, sugar, and salt and pepper to taste. Cover, and simmer for 30 minutes. Add a little water if it cooks down too dry. Add wine. Mix with cooked spaghetti and cheese, put into casserole, and bake slowly (325 degrees F.) for 1 hour.

CREAMED CHIPPED BEEF AND MUSHROOMS, SAUTERNE (*Serves 6*)

6 tbsps. butter or margarine
1 medium onion, minced
1 lb. mushrooms, cleaned and sliced
½ cup Sauterne or Rhine Wine
3 tbsps. flour
1½ cups milk
¼ lb. chipped beef, minced
Pepper to taste

Melt 3 tablespoons butter or margarine. Add the onion, and cook for about 3 minutes. Add the mushrooms and ¼ cup of the wine. Cover, and cook gently for about 8 minutes.

Melt remaining butter or margarine in a saucepan. Add the flour. When smooth, add the milk and cook slowly, stirring constantly, until sauce begins to boil. Then add remaining ¼ cup of wine. Add mushrooms to sauce. Finally, add the minced chipped beef. Add pepper to taste, and serve on toast or over hot biscuits.

TAMALE PIE (*Serves 8 to 10*)

1 cup corn meal
1½ tsps. salt
4 cups boiling water
¼ cup meat fryings
1 large onion, minced
2 cloves garlic, minced
1 lb. hamburger
2 tsps. salt
¼ tsp. pepper
1 to 1½ tbsps. chili powder
2 cups diced fresh or canned tomatoes
1 cup water
1 cup Claret or Burgundy
¼ cup American cheese, grated

Add corn meal and 1½ teaspoons salt slowly to boiling water in double boiler, stirring constantly, until smoothly thickened. Cover, and let cook for 45 minutes. Cool until thick enough to hold its shape. While mush is cooking, fry onion and garlic in meat fryings until limp. Add meat, and cook, stirring, until seared. Add salt, pepper, chili powder, tomatoes, and water, and let simmer for 15 minutes. Add wine and cheese. Taste. Add more seasonings if needed. Line bottom and sides of a greased shallow baking dish with three fourths of the mush. Fill with meat mixture. Drop remaining mush by spoonfuls over the top, and bake in slow oven (325 degrees F.) for 45 minutes.

PORK CHOPS, WHITE WINE (*Serves 6*)

6 pork or veal chops
1 clove garlic or 1 minced onion
Salt, pepper, poultry seasoning
Flour
2 cups Sauterne or Rhine Wine

Have chops cut about ¾ inch thick. Trim off excess fat. Place chops in a deep bowl and cover with wine. Add a sliced clove of garlic or the minced onion. Weigh down meat with a small plate to keep it covered with wine, and let stand in refrigerator for several hours, or overnight. Remove meat, drain, sprinkle with salt and pepper and a bit of poultry seasoning. Roll in flour, and brown well in a small amount of hot shortening. Remove meat from skillet and place in casserole. Pour off fat from skillet. Add the wine in which the chops were marinated. Heat, and pour over chops to cover. Bake in a moderate oven (350 degrees F.) for 45 minutes. Remove cover, increase heat to 400 degrees F., and bake 10 to 15 minutes longer, or until most of the liquid has been evaporated.

PORK CHOPS AND APPLES, CLARET (*Serves 6*)

6 pork chops
Salt, pepper
½ cup Claret or Burgundy
6 apple slices ½ inch thick
2 tbsps. brown sugar

Preheat oven to 400 degrees F. Sprinkle chops with salt and pepper. Arrange in shallow baking dish. Bake until browned on both sides, then top with apple slices. Sprinkle brown sugar over apple slices. Reduce oven temperature to moderate (350 degrees F.). Pour ¼ cup of the wine over the chops. After 10 minutes add remaining wine. Bake 20 minutes longer, basting occasionally with the wine from the bottom of the baking dish.

BAKED PORK CHOPS, WINE CRANBERRY DRESSING (*Serves 6*)

6 pork chops
2 cups cranberries
¼ cup butter, margarine, or bacon fat
½ cup sugar
¾ cup celery, chopped
1 tsp. salt
⅛ tsp. pepper
2 tsps. sage
1 tsp. thyme
3 tbsps. parsley, chopped fine
5 cups toasted bread cubes
1¼ cups Burgundy or Claret

Wipe chops with a damp cloth and sprinkle with salt and pepper. Simmer cranberries in the butter or margarine until the skins begin to break. Add the sugar. Mix celery and seasonings with the bread cubes. Add 1½ cups cranberries, and mix well. Moisten with ½ cup of wine. Form the dressing into a mound in a shallow baking dish.

Brown chops lightly in a skillet. Place them around the mound of dressing. Bake in a moderate oven (350 degrees F.) for 40 minutes. Baste with remaining ¾ cup wine. Arrange chops and dressing on large platter, and serve garnished with fried apple slices and remaining ½ cup cranberries.

ROAST LOIN OF PORK, BURGUNDY

(Serves 8 to 10)

1 4 to 5 lb. pork loin roast
2 cups Claret or Burgundy
2 tbsps. sugar
Salt and pepper
¼ cup flour
¼ cup cold water

Place roast in deep dish. Pour wine over meat and allow to stand in refrigerator overnight. Next morning transfer meat to an uncovered roasting pan. Bake in a moderate oven (350 degrees F.). Pour wine over meat after 30 minutes of roasting. Sprinkle with salt, pepper, and sugar. Baste meat frequently with wine and drippings from bottom of pan. Allow 25 to 30 minutes per pound for large roasts and 40 to 50 minutes per pound for small roasts. (If meat thermometer is used, bake until thermometer registers 185 degrees for inside of roast.)

To prepare gravy, skim excess fat from wine and drippings left in pan. Measure drippings. Add enough water to make 2 cups of liquid. Blend flour with ¼ cup cold water and ½ cup drippings. Add to remaining drippings, and cook, stirring constantly, until gravy is thickened and smooth. Serve with roast.

PORK AND NOODLE CASSEROLE (*Serves 4*)

½ lb. lean pork, cut in strips
2 tbsps. pork fat
3 tbsps. chopped onion
¾ cup chopped celery
Salt and pepper
3 bouillon cubes
1½ cups boiling water
¾ cup Sauterne or Rhine Wine
4 cups cooked noodles
¼ cup sliced stuffed olives

Brown pork strips in fat in hot skillet. Add chopped onion and celery, and fry 5 minutes. Dissolve bouillon cubes in boiling water, combine with pork strips, onion, and celery, and simmer, covered, for 15 minutes. Add wine. Mix with cooked noodles and sliced stuffed olives. Season to taste. Bake in moderate oven (350 degrees F.) for 40 minutes.

CORNED PORK SHOULDER, CLARET (*Serves 10 to 12*)

Corned or pickled pork shoulder, 5 to 6 lbs.
1 cup Claret or Burgundy
Cloves
½ cup brown sugar
1 tbsp. cornstarch
½ tsp. dry mustard

Cover corned or pickled pork shoulder with cold water. Heat to boiling, skim, then turn heat low and simmer, covered, for 2½ to 3 hours, until tender. Let cool in cooking water if convenient. Take out, remove skin and excess fat, score fat, and stick with cloves. Place in baking pan. Pour wine over meat and bake in moderately hot oven (375 degrees F.) for about 40 minutes, basting often with wine in pan. Spread fat with brown sugar which has been mixed with cornstarch and dry mustard, and bake about 20 minutes longer, or until browned and glazed. Serve hot or cold.

BARBECUED SPARERIBS, BURGUNDY
(*Serves 6*)

1 cup Burgundy or Claret
1 garlic clove
¼ cup vinegar
½ cup salad oil
2 onions, grated
3 tomatoes, sieved
5 to 6 pounds spareribs
1 tbsp. brown sugar
1 tbsp. salt
1 tsp. pepper
2 tbsps. Worcestershire sauce
¼ tsp. chili powder
Dash cayenne

Crush garlic in the wine. Add remaining ingredients and mix well. Place spareribs in a large baking pan. Pour on sauce. Bake in a moderately hot oven (375 degrees F.) for 1½ hours, or until ribs are browned. Baste with sauce in bottom of the pan several times during the baking period.

WINE-GLAZED HAM (*Serves 3 to 4*)

1 1-inch thick slice pre-cooked ham
12 whole cloves
2 tbsps. prepared mustard
½ cup brown sugar
1 cup Port, Muscatel or Tokay

Cut gashes into ham fat about 1 inch apart. Stud fat with cloves. Place ham in an open roasting pan, and heat thoroughly in a moderate (350 degrees F.) oven. Allow 20 minutes for heating. Remove ham from oven; spread with mustard and sugar. Raise oven temperature to 400 degrees F. Return ham to oven, and allow 15 to 20 minutes for glazing. Spoon the wine over the ham at intervals during the glazing period.

NOTE: *For regular smoked ham, bake 25 to 30 minutes per pound at 325 degrees F. before glazing.*

HAM STEAK WITH PORT WINE APPLES
(*Serves 6*)

1 thick slice precooked ham, about 2 lbs.
12 whole cloves
¾ cup brown sugar
¾ cup Port
4 apples

Cut gashes into ham fat about 1 inch apart. Stud fat with cloves. Place ham in an open roasting pan, and heat thoroughly in a 350-degree F. oven. Allow 25 to 30 minutes for heating. Remove ham from oven. Spread with sugar and pour wine over ham slice slowly. Set oven at 400 degrees F. Return ham to oven and allow 15 to 20 minutes for glazing. Remove ham to hot platter. Core and slice the apples. Cook apple slices in wine and sugar syrup left in roasting pan for about 5 minutes, turning once.

NOTE: *For regular smoked ham, bake 25 to 30 minutes per pound at 325 degrees F. before glazing.*

BAKED HAM, SHERRY GLAZE AND SHERRY RAISIN SAUCE (*Serves 12*)

1 half ham
24 whole cloves
1 cup brown sugar
2 cups Sherry
1 cup raisins
1 cup water
¼ cup granulated sugar
1 tbsp. cornstarch
1 tsp. mustard
1 tsp. salt

Bake ham on open roasting rack in moderately low oven (325 degrees F.), allowing 22 minutes per pound, or to an internal temperature of 150 degrees. (Precooked ham needs only to be heated before glazing.) Set oven temperature to moderately hot (400 degrees F.). Remove the skin and score the surface of the ham. Stud with cloves. Slowly pour ½ cup of the wine over the surface of the ham. Rub with brown sugar, and bake 10 minutes. Drip another ½ cup wine over the sugared ham surface very slowly. Return to oven for another 5 to 10 minutes, or until ham is glazed.

Cook raisins in water for 10 minutes. Drain, but save the water in which raisins have cooked. Blend cornstarch, sugar, mustard, and salt with raisin water, and cook, stirring constantly, until thickened and clear. Add the raisins and the remaining 1 cup of wine. Heat to boiling.

BAKED HAM AND LIMA BEAN CASSEROLE
(*Serves 8*)

- 3 cups Lima beans
- ¼ cup butter or margarine
- ½ lb. smoked ham, cut in cubes
- 2 onions, sliced
- 1 green pepper, cut in strips
- 2 tsps. salt
- ¼ cup brown sugar
- ½ tsp. mustard
- ½ tsp. Worcestershire sauce
- 1 cup stock
- 1½ cups Sauterne or Rhine Wine
- 2 tbsps. flour
- 2 tbsps. butter or margarine

If dried Lima beans are used, soak overnight; drain, cover with fresh water, and cook slowly until skins break.

Brown the ham cubes, sliced onions, and strips of green pepper in the butter or margarine. Mix through beans. Make a sauce by combining salt, sugar, mustard, Worcestershire sauce, stock, and 1 cup of wine. Blend flour and the remaining 2 tablespoons butter or margarine and add to sauce. Cook until it thickens slightly. Mix with beans and ham.

Turn into bean pot or casserole, and bake, covered, in

a 300-degree F. oven for 4 hours. Add remaining wine, and bake 1 hour longer. Sprinkle additional brown sugar over top of beans about 15 minutes before removing from oven, to add a glaze.

NOTE: *When canned or parboiled fresh Lima beans are used, reduce stock to ½ cup and wine to ¾ cup in making the sauce. Parboil ham cubes with beans. Bake only 30 minutes for glaze.*

BARBECUED LAMB CUBES (*Serves 5 to 6*)

1½ lbs. lean lamb
2 onions, sliced
2 tsps. salt
2 tbsps. salad oil
¼ tsp. pepper
½ tsp. oregano or rosemary
½ cup Sherry

Cut meat into inch cubes. Mix with onions, seasonings, wine, and salad oil, and let stand in refrigerator several hours, or overnight. Remove meat, place on metal skewers, 3 or 4 to a skewer, and broil over the hot coals of the barbecue, or in the broiling oven.

BAKED LAMB CHOPS (*Serves 6*)

6 shoulder lamb chops
1 clove garlic
Salt and pepper
2 tbsps. cooking fat
2 medium onions, chopped
2 cups cooked carrots, diced
4 tbsps. flour
4 tbsps. chili sauce
½ cup Sauterne or Rhine Wine

Rub chops with cut clove of garlic; sprinkle with salt and pepper. Brown on both sides in hot fat in frying pan. Remove to baking dish. Sauté onions and carrots in pan until onions are soft. Add flour, chili sauce, and wine, and cook until thickened. Place a mound of carrot mixture on top of each chop and bake in moderate oven (350 degrees F.) for 45 minutes.

LAMB STEW, SAUTERNE (*Serves 4 to 5*)

2 lbs. lean lamb shoulder
2 onions, sliced
1 to 2 cloves garlic, peeled
1½ cups Sauterne or Rhine Wine
3 cups water
Vegetables
¼ cup flour
1 tsp. salt
¼ tsp. pepper
¼ cup oil

Cut lamb into 2-inch cubes and place in deep bowl with onions and garlic. Add wine, cover, and let stand in refrigerator for 2 or 3 hours. Discard garlic. Take out meat, roll in seasoned flour, brown in hot oil in kettle. Add wine, onions, and water. Cover, and simmer until tender—about 1½ hours. Add vegetables—carrots, potatoes, celery, small whole onions, and peas as desired. Season well, and cook until tender—about 20 minutes.

ROAST LAMB SHANKS, CLARET (*Serves 4*)

4 meaty lamb shanks
Celery tops
Parsley
1 bay leaf
½ cup oil
1 clove garlic
Salt and pepper
½ cup flour
1 cup Claret or Burgundy

Put lamb shanks into a kettle with a few celery tops, a sprig of parsley, bay leaf, a sprig of thyme or rosemary, and a bit of garlic if desired. Add boiling water, barely enough to cover meat, and cook gently for 1 hour, adding 1½ teaspoons salt and ¼ teaspoon pepper toward end of cooking time. Remove shanks from broth, sprinkle with salt and pepper. Roll in flour, and place in shallow baking pan. Roast in moderate oven (375 degrees F.) for about 1 hour, or until crisply browned, turning occasionally and basting frequently with wine mixed with oil. When done, make gravy in roasting pan, using strained broth in which shanks were cooked.

LEG OF LAMB, SAUTERNE (*Serves 6 to 8*)

1 leg of lamb, 5 to 7 lbs.
Salt and pepper
2 cups Sauterne or Rhine Wine

Wipe leg of lamb with damp cloth. Sprinkle with salt and pepper. Put meat on a rack in an open roasting pan, and place in moderate oven (325 degrees F.), allowing 35 minutes per pound for 3- to 5-pound roast; 30 minutes per pound for 6- to 8-pound roast. If a meat thermometer is used, place in thickest part of meat, and bake until it registers 180 degrees F.

Pour the wine over the lamb at beginning of baking period. It will gather in roasting pan and should be used to baste the lamb frequently. During the baking period the lamb may be pricked with a baking fork frequently to allow more of the wine to penetrate the meat. Serve with gravy made from drippings and wine.

ROAST LAMB SHOULDER, RED WINE MINT SAUCE (*Serves 4 to 5*)

1 shoulder cut of lamb, 3-4 lbs.
Salt and pepper
2 cups Claret or Burgundy
1 bunch fresh mint
2 tbsps. lemon juice
1 tsp. sugar
1 cup stock

Rub roast with salt and pepper. Arrange on open roasting rack and roast at 300 to 350 degrees F. until thermometer registers 175 degrees, or allow about 30 minutes per pound. Baste occasionally with 1 cup of the wine.

Prepare mint sauce by heating stock, adding remaining one cup of wine, sugar, lemon juice, salt and pepper to taste, and ¼ cup chopped fresh mint leaves. Serve hot with lamb.

MIXED GRILL IN CLARET *(Serves 4)*

4 thick lamb chops
4 thick slices liverwurst
4 thick slices unpeeled orange
½ tsp. sugar
4 cooked potato halves
1 cup Claret or Burgundy

Brush meats, orange, and potato with butter or margarine. Make a wine sauce by heating 2 tablespoons butter or margarine and 1 tablespoon flour; stir in wine and sugar; season with salt, pepper, and herbs. Broil chops until brown on one side, basting with the hot wine sauce. Turn, put in other items, and broil, basting meats frequently with the sauce until done. Pour any remaining sauce from broiler pan over mixed grill.

BROILED LAMB CHOPS, SHERRY MARINADE *(Serves 4 to 6)*

6 loin or rib lamb chops, 1″ thick
1 tsp. dry mustard
1 tsp. salt
½ tsp. pepper
½ cup Sherry
½ clove garlic, minced, or 1 large onion, minced

Trim excess fat from chops and keep for use in oiling broiler rack or frying pan. Arrange chops in shallow pan.

Combine mustard, salt, pepper, Sherry, and garlic or onion. Rub marinade into chops on both sides. Pour remaining marinade over chops. Cover, and set in refrigerator for about 3 hours. Remove from refrigerator about 40 minutes before broiling chops. Have broiler rack 3 inches from flame. Set oven control to very hot (500 to 550 degrees F.) and preheat broiler 10 minutes. Rub broiler rack with lamb fat cut from chops. Arrange chops on broiler rack, and broil 7 to 8 minutes on each side. Baste with marinade left in refrigerator pan.

Place chops on preheated platter. Pour drippings from broiler pan over chops. Broil or pan fry orange slices sprinkled lightly with Sherry and brown sugar. Orange slices will be lightly browned in 1 to 2 minutes. Serve with chops.

VEAL CHOPS, SAUTERNE (*Serves 6*)

- 6 veal kidney or rib chops
- Salt and pepper
- 6 tbsps. cooking oil or bacon fat
- 1 onion, minced
- ½ lb. whole mushrooms
- 1¼ cups Sauterne or Rhine Wine
- 12 carrots
- 2 tbsps. brown sugar

Sprinkle chops with salt and pepper. Brown well in ¼ cup hot oil or bacon fat. Cook onion and mushrooms in remaining 2 tablespoons hot oil or bacon fat. Add wine to chops and simmer, covered, for 25 minutes. Add mushrooms to one side of pan and carrots to the other. Cook for 20 minutes. Sprinkle carrots and mushrooms with salt and pepper. Sprinkle brown sugar over carrots. Cook, uncovered, for 5 minutes until carrots are glazed. Remove meat and vegetables to platter.

To make a gravy, add 1 cup water to drippings left in pan. Allow to boil for 1 minute. Shake 1 tablespoon flour in a covered jar with ¼ cup warm water. Cook until slightly thickened. Season with salt and pepper as desired.

VEAL SCALLOPINI (*Serves 4 to 5*)

1 lb. veal cutlet, sliced ¼″ thick
Flour
Salt, pepper
2 tbsps. oil
1 clove garlic, crushed
½ cup Sauterne or Rhine Wine
½ cup water
2 tsps. lemon juice

Cut meat into small pieces and roll in seasoned flour. Heat oil with garlic in heavy frying pan, and brown the floured meat. Remove garlic; add wine, water, and lemon juice. Cover, and let simmer for about 30 minutes, or until meat is very tender. A pinch of marjoram or thyme may be added while cooking.

VEAL À LA KING (*Serves 8*)

2 cups cooked or leftover roast veal, cut in cubes
1 cup chicken broth
1½ cups rich milk
½ cup butter or margarine
5 tbsps. flour
½ tsp. salt
1½ cups mushrooms, sliced
3 tbsps. green pepper, chopped
2 egg yolks
⅓ cup Sherry
Patty shells or toast points
2 tbsps. pimiento, cut in strips

Melt ¼ cup butter or margarine; blend in the flour. Add hot chicken broth and the milk, and cook slowly, stirring constantly, until mixture is thick. Add salt and the cubed veal.

Sauté the mushrooms and green pepper in the remaining ¼ cup butter or margarine and add to à la king mixture. Pour hot mixture over beaten egg yolks and return to fire and cook 1 minute, stirring constantly. Add pimiento and the wine. Serve hot in patty shells or on toast points.

VEAL CUTLETS, SAUTERNE (*Serves 6*)

6 veal cutlets
Flour
Salt and pepper
Cooking fat
½ lb. fresh mushrooms, cut in small pieces
Chopped parsley
1 or 2 cloves garlic, chopped fine
1 cup Sauterne or Rhine Wine
4 tomatoes, diced, or
2 cups solid-pack canned

Dip cutlets in seasoned flour and fry in plenty of cooking fat until nicely browned. Put in mushrooms, and let simmer 4 or 5 minutes. Add remaining ingredients; season to taste. Cover, and let simmer 20 to 30 minutes longer.

APPLE FRANKFURTERS AND SAUERKRAUT, SAUTERNE (*Serves 5 to 6*)

1 lb. frankfurters
¼ cup cooking fat
1½ pts. sauerkraut, drained
1 onion, minced
3 apples, peeled and sliced
2 cups Sauterne or Rhine Wine
2 tbsps. brown sugar
1 large potato

Split frankfurters in half lengthwise, or slice in 1-inch rounds. Brown in the cooking fat in a large skillet. Set aside while cooking sauerkraut. Add sauerkraut to cooking fat left in skillet. Add minced onion, sliced apples, the wine, and the sugar. Cover, and simmer over very low heat until the liquid is reduced by half. Grate the potato and add to the sauerkraut. Top with sliced frankfurters, and bake or simmer for about 15 minutes longer, or until the potato has cooked and thickened the juices.

KIDNEY SAUTÉ (*Serves 2 to 3*)

1 lb. kidneys (2 veal, 3 pork, or 5 lamb)	Salt and pepper
1 medium onion, chopped	2 tbsps. flour
2 tbsps. margarine or oil	½ cup Burgundy or Claret
	½ cup water

Slice kidneys; remove white tubes. Soak in cold salted water for 15 minutes. Fry onion in margarine or oil until limp. Add drained kidneys, and brown well. Sprinkle with salt, pepper, and flour, and brown lightly, stirring. Add wine and water, and cook, stirring, until smooth. Cover, and simmer for 10 to 15 minutes, or until kidneys are tender.

BRAISED BEEF LIVER, SHERRY (*Serves 6*)

1½ lbs. beef liver	¼ cup bacon fat
¼ cup flour	1 cup water
1 tsp. salt	1 cup Sherry
¼ tsp. pepper	2 tbsps. parsley, chopped

Wash liver. Dry. Mix flour, salt, and pepper. Dip liver in flour mixture. Sauté liver in hot bacon fat until browned on both sides. Add ½ cup water and ½ cup Sherry. Cover, and simmer slowly for 15 minutes. Add remaining Sherry, and cook 5 minutes. Serve sprinkled with chopped parsley. Add remaining ½ cup water to gravy left in pan. Thicken with more flour if desired.

BRAISED LIVER, WHITE WINE (*Serves 6*)

- 1½ lbs. beef or pork liver, sliced thin
- 1 cup Sauterne or Rhine Wine
- ¼ cup flour
- 1 tsp. salt
- ¼ tsp. pepper
- 3 tbsps. butter or margarine
- 2 tbsps. fat
- 1½ cups water

Wash liver. Let stand in wine for about ½ hour. Remove from wine, reserving wine for later use. Roll liver in flour to which salt and pepper have been added. Brown on both sides in hot fat and butter or margarine. Add the wine, cover, and simmer for 3 minutes. Add the water, and continue simmering for 15 minutes. Serve in gravy.

LIVER-AND-RICE CASSEROLE (*Serves 6*)

- 2 tbsps. cooking oil
- 3 large onions
- 1 tsp. paprika
- Dash cayenne
- Salt and pepper
- 1 cup brown rice, uncooked
- 2 cups canned bouillon
- 6 slices bacon
- ½ lb. lamb's liver
- 2 tbsps. flour
- ½ cup water
- 1 cup Sauterne or Rhine Wine
- 1 tbsp. lemon juice

Put oil in frying pan over low flame. Slice onions into it, add seasonings, and washed, drained rice. Cook slowly for 10 minutes, or until rice begins to pop. Add 1 cup bouillon; cook until dry; then add remaining bouillon a little at a time, and let cook dry after each addition. Stir constantly to prevent burning. Fry bacon in another pan until half done; drain on paper. Fry floured liver in bacon fat until browned on both sides but not thoroughly cooked. Place most of cooked rice in casserole; put liver on top of it; cover with remaining rice. Make gravy by stirring 2 tablespoons flour into fat remaining in pan after frying liver. When browned, add water and wine, and cook, stirring, until smoothly thickened. Add lemon juice and more seasonings if needed. Pour gravy over rice and liver, cover, and bake in a moderate oven (350 degrees F.) for 30 minutes. Remove cover, top with bacon. Replace in oven until bacon is crisp.

SAUTÉED LIVER, WHITE WINE (*Serves 6*)

1½ lbs. calves' liver sliced ½ inch thick
¼ cup flour
1 tsp. salt
¼ tsp. pepper
2 tbsps. fat
3 tbsps. butter or margarine
1 cup Sauterne or Rhine Wine
1 cup water

Wipe liver with damp cloth. Roll in flour to which salt and pepper have been added. Sauté in hot fat and butter or margarine for 5 to 8 minutes, until browned on both sides. Add ½ cup of the wine. Cover, and simmer for 3 minutes. Remove liver to hot platter. Add remaining wine and water to juices left in pan, and cook slowly, stirring constantly, until gravy is thickened and smooth—about 5 minutes.

LIVER AND ONIONS, BURGUNDY (*Serves 4*)

8 thin slices liver (¾ to 1 lb.)
½ cup Burgundy or Claret
4 medium onions, sliced
6 tbsps. oil or meat fryings

Add wine to sliced liver (calf, beef, lamb, or pork). Let stand in refrigerator an hour or longer, turning occasionally. About ½ hour before serving time fry sliced onions in part of fat until lightly browned. Remove, and keep hot. Add remaining fat to skillet. Drain liver slices, roll in seasoned flour, brown quickly in same skillet, adding more fat if needed. (Allow about 10 minutes for cooking liver.) Take up and keep hot. To skillet add 1 teaspoon flour, blend well, then stir in wine in which the liver was marinated, and cook, stirring, until smooth and slightly thickened. Season to taste. Serve on hot platter, pouring wine gravy over all.

OXTAIL STEW (*Serves 4 to 6*)

2 oxtails (about 2 lbs.) cut into joints	2 cups water
¼ cup meat fryings	1 cup Claret or Burgundy
Salt and pepper	8 small onions
	½ cup sliced celery
1 bay leaf	6 to 8 carrots, diced

Brown oxtails on all sides in meat fryings. Sprinkle with salt and pepper, add bay leaf, water, and wine. Simmer 3 to 4 hours, or until tender, adding more water as necessary. Add vegetables, and cook for 20 to 30 minutes longer. Take up meat and vegetables; thicken gravy with flour-and-water paste.

TONGUE IN RED WINE JELLY (*Serves 4*)

½ lb. boiled tongue, chilled and sliced	½ cup cold water
	1 qt. beef consommé
3 tbsps. unflavored gelatin	¼ cup Claret or Burgundy

Soak the gelatin in cold water. Heat the consommé, and dissolve gelatin in hot consommé. Cool slightly, and add the wine. Rinse a ring mold in cold water. Pour ½ cup of the consommé mixture into ring mold. Chill until it begins to thicken slightly. Arrange slices of the tongue in bottom of ring mold. Pour 1 cup of consommé over slices of tongue. Chill until it begins to congeal. Add remaining sliced tongue and remaining consommé mixture. Chill until congealed. Unmold, and serve on bed of lettuce or water cress.

SPICED TONGUE, BURGUNDY (*Serves 6 to 8*)

1 beef or veal tongue, fresh, 2 to 3 lbs.
2 cups Burgundy or Claret
2 cups water or stock
½ tsp. allspice
12 whole cloves
Lemon slices
2 bay leaves
1 medium onion, minced
2 carrots
½ cup celery, chopped
1 cup raisins

Scrub tongue, place in kettle, and cover with boiling water. Add small amount of salt to water. Cook for about 2 hours. Skin the tongue and remove the root ends. Heat wine and stock. Add spices, carrots, celery, onion, and raisins, and cook 1 hour longer. Serve tongue sliced on platter garnished with onion rings, carrots, and water cress. Thicken wine-stock mixture for gravy. Add small amount of sugar and lemon juice to suit taste. Garnish with lemon slices.

BORDELAISE SAUCE

4 tbsps. butter or margarine
2 tbsps. onion, minced
2 tbsps. green pepper, minced
2 tbsps. flour
1 cup meat stock
¾ cup tomato purée
½ cup Claret or Burgundy
¼ cup stuffed olives, chopped

Brown the onion and green pepper in the butter or margarine. Add the flour and meat stock. Cook until slightly thickened. Add the tomato purée and the wine. Just before serving add chopped olives. Serve with meat, fish, or fowl.

WINE BARBECUE SAUCE

- ½ cup Claret or Burgundy
- 2 tbsps. vinegar
- ½ cup salad oil
- 1 large onion, grated
- 1 clove garlic, crushed
- 2 tsps. salt
- ½ tsp. pepper
- Dash cayenne and a pinch of thyme, marjoram, or rosemary

Combine ingredients in order given, stirring until the salt is dissolved. Let stand several hours, or overnight. Use to baste or brush over broiling chickens, steaks, chops, applying frequently and generously during the broiling period. This sauce may be kept for several days, in which case it is best to remove the garlic after the first 24 hours.

BEARNAISE SAUCE

- 2 tbsps. chives, chopped fine
- 1 shallot, chopped fine
- ½ cup Sauterne or Rhine Wine
- 3 egg yolks
- ¼ lb. butter or margarine
- 2 tbsps. parsley, chopped

Simmer the chives and the shallot in the wine until the wine has evaporated to approximately half the original amount. Beat the egg yolks until thick and light, and place them in a double boiler. Add the chives and shallot in wine and the butter or margarine (1 tablespoon at a time), beating the mixture with a wire whip all the while. Cook slowly, until sauce thickens to the consistency of mayonnaise. Add parsley before serving. Serve with steak, any grilled meat, or fish. (If the sauce tends to separate in the cooking process, remove from over hot water, add 1 teaspoon cold water, and heat well.)

CUMBERLAND SAUCE

3 tbsps. red currant jelly
2 tbsps. Port
2 tbsps. orange juice
1 tbsp. lemon juice
1 tsp. dry English mustard
1 tsp. paprika
½ tsp. ground ginger
3 tbsps. orange rind, finely shredded

Melt jelly over low flame until liquid. Add other ingredients and simmer for 2 minutes. Let stand for an hour or more before serving. Serve over duck, venison, cold cuts, or ham.

SHERRY MUSHROOM SAUCE

½ cup Sherry
1 cup sliced mushrooms
2 cups meat stock
Salt and pepper to taste
2 tbsps. butter or margarine
2 tbsps. flour

Cook the mushrooms in the wine until the wine is reduced to half the original amount. Melt the butter or margarine, add the flour, and blend until smooth. Gradually add the meat stock, and cook, stirring constantly, until mixture becomes thick and smooth. Season to taste with salt and pepper. Add the mushrooms and wine, and serve very hot. Serve on meats.

CHAPTER 10

POULTRY AND GAME

Wine is as good as life to man if it be drunk
moderately;
What is life to man that is without wine?
For it was made to make man glad.

ECCLESIASTICUS, CH. 31, V. 27

Chicken and turkey find natural flavor-mates among the white table wines, such as Sauterne and Rhine Wine; here, as with sea food, the more delicate food flavors appear to harmonize best with the lighter wine flavors. Sherry enjoys wide popularity in the cooking of these foods, too, and lends a highly distinctive nutlike flavor.

Game, with its heartier flavor, usually calls for the more full-bodied red table wines, such as Claret and Burgundy. These wines are almost universally favored in the preparation of venison, or for serving with this meat.

CHICKEN FRICASSEE, RHINE WINE (*Serves 6*)

- 1 4-lb. chicken, cut for fricassee
- 2 tsps. salt
- 2 cups water
- 1½ cups Rhine Wine or Sauterne
- 2 carrots, sliced
- 3 sprigs parsley
- ¼ cup celery, chopped
- 2 slices onion
- 3 tbsps. flour
- 3 egg yolks
- ⅓ cup cream

Arrange chicken in stewing kettle. Pour on water and 1 cup of the wine. Add salt, carrots, parsley, celery, and onion, and cook slowly until chicken is very tender—about 2 hours. Remove chicken to platter. Strain broth and skim off excess fat. Measure. Add remaining ½ cup wine and enough water to make 2 cups liquid. Heat to boiling. Shake flour with cream in a covered jar until blended and smooth. Add to hot broth. Cook, stirring constantly, until thickened and smooth.

Season with salt and pepper to taste. Beat egg yolks. Pour small amount of hot mixture into beaten egg yolks gradually, stirring all the while. Add to hot gravy. Cook 1 minute. Add chicken to gravy. Heat thoroughly. Serve chicken with rice or dumplings. Spoon gravy over chicken. Serve remaining gravy from gravy boat.

CHICKEN SAUTÉ, WHITE WINE CREAM GRAVY (*Serves 8*)

2 3-lb. frying chickens
Flour
Salt, pepper
2 tbsps. parsley, minced
2 tbsps. chives, minced
¾ cup Sauterne or Rhine Wine
1½ cups sour cream
Butter and bacon fat for browning

Separate the chicken into serving pieces. Dredge in flour to which salt and pepper have been added. Brown in hot butter and bacon fat. Add ½ cup of the wine and sprinkle chopped parsley and chives over browned chicken. Cover, and cook the chicken until tender (about 40 minutes). Remove chicken and arrange on hot platter. Add remaining ¼ cup wine to the juices in the pan and stir in the sour cream. Serve garnished with parsley and spiced fruit.

SHERRIED CHICKEN IN CASSEROLE
(*Serves 4 to 6*)

1 frying chicken, 3 to 4 lbs.
Salt, pepper, flour
¼ cup oil
1 cup diced celery
2 tbsps. minced onion
1 tbsp. flour
¼ cup Sherry
¾ cup thin cream or top milk

Cut up chicken, sprinkle with salt and pepper. Flour lightly, and fry slowly in oil. Transfer to a casserole. Add celery, onion, and 1 tablespoon flour to oil in skillet; stir over low heat for 2 minutes. Season lightly, and add to chicken. Add wine and cream or top milk. Cover, and bake in moderate oven (350 degrees F.) for 30 to 45 minutes, or until tender.

ROAST CHICKEN, SAUTERNE (*Serves 4 to 6*)

1 4-lb. roasting chicken
3 cups stuffing
Salt and poultry seasoning
¼ cup butter or margarine
1 cup Sauterne or Rhine Wine

Singe, clean, and wash the chicken. Dry thoroughly inside and outside with a clean towel. Rub inside of fowl with salt, allowing about ⅛ teaspoon salt for each pound of chicken. Fill lightly with bread and celery stuffing, allowing some room for the stuffing to expand during cooking. Place a small amount of dressing in the neck to round out the contour. Close by sewing with needle and thread, or insert skewers and lace with string. Truss. Place chicken breast side down in an uncovered roasting pan. Cover with cloth saturated with fat, and bake in moderate oven (325 degrees F.) for about 1 hour. Turn chicken breast side up. Cover with same cloth and bake

1 to 1½ hours longer. Remove cloth for last half hour to permit deeper browning. Baste at intervals during baking time with the melted butter or margarine and the wine. Allow 30 to 35 minutes per pound for a 4- to 5-pound chicken. Prepare gravy from wine-flavored drippings in bottom of pan.

Bread and Celery Stuffing for Roast Chicken
(Makes 3 cups stuffing)

1½ cups bread crumbs
1 cup celery, finely chopped
½ tsp. salt
⅛ tsp. pepper
¾ tsp. thyme or marjoram
½ onion, minced
3 tbsps. butter or margarine
1 egg, beaten

Mix bread crumbs, celery, seasonings, and onion. Add the melted butter or margarine and the beaten egg. Mix lightly with a fork. Stuff bird lightly. Do not pack.

BROILED CHICKEN, SAUTERNE *(Serves 4)*

2 small fryers, 1½ lbs. each
1 small onion, sliced
1 cup cold water
1 cup Sauterne or Rhine Wine
2 tbsps. oil
Parsley
Lemon juice
1 clove garlic
Salt and pepper
1 tbsp. butter or margarine
1 tbsp. flour

Have fryers split for broiling. Cut off necks and put with giblets in saucepan with onion and sprig of parsley; add cold water, cover, and let simmer until tender. Add wine, and strain. This sauce is to be used for basting during broiling.

Chop giblets fine and set aside. Rub chickens with cut clove of garlic, sprinkle with lemon juice, salt, and pepper. Brush with oil, and place skin side down in shallow pan. Place low under broiler. Turn occasionally, and baste frequently with the wine sauce. When chickens are tender and well browned (about 30 minutes), remove from pan. Thicken remaining sauce slightly with 1 tablespoon flour and butter or margarine rubbed together. Add chopped giblets, heat, and pour a little of the sauce over each serving of chicken.

CHICKEN MUSHROOM LOAF (*Serves 8*)

3 cups cooked roast chicken
3 cups soft bread crumbs
½ cup celery, chopped
¼ cup Sherry
3 eggs
2 tsps. salt
2 tsps. parsley, minced

Mix ingredients well. Pack into greased loaf pan and bake in a moderate oven (350 degrees F.) for about 40 minutes. Unmold, and serve with mushroom sauce. To prepare sauce, add ¼ cup Sherry to one can cream of mushroom soup and heat.

CHICKEN A LA KING (*Serves 8*)

2 cups cooked or leftover chicken, cut in cubes
1 cup chicken broth
1½ cups rich milk
½ cup butter or margarine
5 tbsps. flour
½ tsp. salt
1½ cups mushrooms, sliced
3 tbsps. green pepper, chopped
2 egg yolks
⅓ cup Sherry
Patty shells or toast points
2 tbsps. pimiento, cut in strips

Melt ¼ cup butter or margarine; blend in the flour. Add hot chicken broth and the milk, and cook slowly, stirring constantly, until mixture is thick. Add salt and the cubed chicken.

Sauté the mushrooms and green pepper in the remaining ¼ cup butter or margarine and add to à la king mixture. Pour hot mixture over beaten egg yolks, and return to fire and cook 1 minute, stirring constantly. Add pimiento and the wine. Serve hot in patty shells or on toast points.

ITALIAN CHICKEN (*Serves 4*)

1 frying chicken, 2 to 3 lbs.
¼ cup butter or oil
Salt and pepper
¼ cup onion, minced
1 cup celery, chopped
¾ cup canned or diced fresh tomatoes
1 tsp. sugar
¾ cup Sauterne or Rhine Wine

Cut chicken into pieces for frying. Wipe dry. Brown in melted fat in skillet. Sprinkle with salt and pepper while cooking. When browned, add onion and celery, and cook until onion is soft. Add tomatoes, sugar, and the wine. Cover, and simmer for 40 minutes.

CHICKEN MARENGO (*Serves 4*)

1 3- to 4-lb. chicken, jointed
Cooking fat or oil
Salt, pepper, thyme
6 green onions, chopped
1¼ cups chicken broth
¾ cup Sauterne or Rhine Wine
2 tbsps. tomato paste
1 tbsp. flour

Heat 1 inch melted cooking fat in skillet or frying pan. Dry chicken pieces, and fry to golden brown on both sides. Season with salt, pepper, and thyme. Transfer to baking dish. Sprinkle with chopped onions. Add ½ cup chicken broth, and bake, uncovered, in a moderate oven (325 degrees F.) for 30 minutes. Add ½ cup wine and the tomato paste. Cover, and bake 20 minutes longer. Uncover, and bake 10 minutes. Remove chicken to hot platter. Add remaining broth and wine to drippings in pan. Shake flour with ¼ cup cold water and add to gravy. Cook until slightly thickened. Serve sauce over chicken.

SHERRIED CHICKEN CUSTARDS (*Serves 6*)

- ¾ cup strong chicken broth
- 1 cup rich milk
- ¼ cup Sherry
- 6 egg yolks, or 3 eggs, beaten
- 1½ tsps. salt
- 2 cups diced cooked chicken

Scald broth, milk, and wine. Stir into egg yolks or beaten eggs, add salt and diced chicken, and pour into greased custard cups. Set cups in pan of hot water, and bake in moderate oven (350 degrees F.) for 40 minutes, or until a knife inserted in the center comes out clean. Serve hot in custard cups.

INDIVIDUAL CHICKEN PIES, WHITE WINE
(*Makes 6 individual pies*)

- 6 medium carrots
- 6 small onions
- 1 medium bunch celery
- ¼ cup butter, margarine, or chicken fat
- ¼ cup flour
- 1 cup chicken stock
- 1 cup milk
- ½ cup Sauterne or Rhine Wine
- ¾ tsp. salt
- Pepper
- 4 cups cooked chicken meat, cut in pieces
- Rich pastry

Cut up the vegetables, and cook them in salted water. Drain. Melt fat in a saucepan, blend in flour, and add chicken stock and milk. Cook until the mixture boils and thickens, stirring constantly. Add the wine, salt, and pepper. Fold in the vegetables and chicken meat. Pour the mixture into six individual casseroles. Cover each one with pastry. Bake in a hot oven (450 degrees F.) for 15 minutes, or until the pastry browns. Serve hot in the casseroles.

CHICKEN OR TURKEY CROQUETTES (*Serves 4 to 6*)

- 6 cups white bread crumbs, soft
- ½ cup celery tops, chopped
- 3 tbsps. onion, minced
- 1½ cups chicken or turkey, cooked and chopped
- 1 tsp. salt
- ¼ tsp. pepper
- ½ tsp. poultry seasoning
- ½ cup Sauterne or Rhine Wine
- 2 tbsps. margarine, melted
- 1 egg, beaten

Mix ingredients in order given. Form into croquettes; place on greased shallow pan; brush with melted margarine. Bake in hot oven (450 degrees F.) for about 25 minutes, or until lightly browned.

CHICKEN OR TURKEY TETRAZZINI, SAUTERNE (*Serves 5 to 6*)

- ½ lb. spaghetti
- ½ cup sliced mushrooms
- 3 tbsps. butter or margarine
- 3 tbsps. flour
- ¾ cup consommé
- ¾ cup Sauterne or Rhine Wine
- ½ cup evaporated milk
- 1½ cups leftover chicken or turkey, cubed

Cook spaghetti in salted water until tender. Drain, and rinse with hot water. Cook mushrooms in butter or margarine for 5 minutes. Sprinkle with flour; stir; add consommé and wine. Cook, stirring, until smooth. Add evaporated milk and season to taste. In a greased baking dish put a layer of spaghetti, then a layer of turkey, and a layer of mushroom sauce. Repeat, ending with a top layer of spaghetti. Sprinkle top generously with buttered bread crumbs mixed with grated Parmesan cheese. Bake in hot oven (450 degrees F.) until lightly browned and bubbling.

ROAST TURKEY, WHITE WINE

(*Serves 14 to 20*)

1 14- to 18-lb. turkey
1 large loaf stale bread
⅓ cup bacon fat
2 medium onions
2 cups celery, chopped
¼ cup parsley, minced
2 eggs, beaten until light
¼ cup flour
1½ tsps. salt
½ tsp. each pepper, powdered thyme, marjoram, and sage
1 cup butter or margarine
2 cups Sauterne or Rhine Wine

Remove pin feathers from turkey. Singe. Wash thoroughly inside and outside with clear, cold water. Rub inside with salt, using ⅛ teaspoon salt, or less, for each pound of turkey. Prepare dressing as follows:

Cover bread with cold water. Soak until soft. Squeeze dry. Brown onion in bacon fat. Add onion, celery, parsley, beaten eggs, salt, pepper, thyme, marjoram, and sage to bread. Mix until light.

Stuff neck of turkey. Fasten skin to back with skewers or sew with needle and thread. Stuff cavity lightly. Fasten with skewers or sew. Fold wings back and press tips against the back. Tie ends of legs together with string and cross string around tailpiece. Turn bird on breast and bring ends of string forward over the wings. Tie in the middle of the back. Lay in pan on a rack, preferably on one side of breast. Roast in a low oven (300 degrees F.) for 15 to 18 minutes per pound, or for a total of 4 to 4½ hours. After 1 hour of roasting, turn bird over to opposite side of breast. When turkey is half done, turn on back. Baste at intervals throughout roasting period with mixture of warm wine and melted butter or margarine. Turkey is done when leg joint breaks or moves readily when drumstick is moved up and down.

Cook giblets to tenderness in salted water. Add liver during last 15 minutes of cooking. Cut giblets fine for adding to gravy.

Prepare gravy as follows: Pour meat juices into a bowl. Skim off as much of the fat as possible. Measure ¼ cup of fat and turn into saucepan. Add the ¼ cup flour to fat, and cook over low heat until frothy. Measure liquid. Add water to make 2½ cups. Add cold liquid to flour mixture all at once. Cook, stirring constantly, until thickened. Boil 5 minutes. Season to taste. Add giblets. Serve hot.

TURKEY LOAF (*Serves 4 to 5*)

2 cups leftover turkey
2 cups soft bread crumbs
¼ cup celery, chopped fine
⅓ cup Sherry
2 tbsps. cream
3 egg yolks
1 tsp. salt
1 tsp. onion, minced

Cut turkey into very small pieces. Add bread crumbs and chopped celery. Beat egg yolks. Add the wine and the cream to egg yolks. Add salt and minced onion. Mix lightly. Pack into greased loaf pan, and bake in a moderate oven (350 degrees F.) for about 40 minutes. Serve with giblet gravy or cheese sauce.

BURGUNDY ROAST DUCK, PRUNE RAISIN STUFFING (*Serves 8*)

2 5-lb. ducks
1½ cups apple, chopped
1 cup white raisins
1 cup prunes, cut in pieces
⅓ cup sugar
2 cups bread crumbs
1 tsp. salt
¼ tsp. pepper
½ tsp. powdered sage
½ tsp. powdered thyme
½ cup orange juice
1½ cups Burgundy or Claret

Remove pin feathers, singe, and wash ducks thoroughly inside and outside with clear, cold water. Dry. Arrange on an open roasting pan, breast side up. Prick skin into the fat layers around tail and over body. Roast in a moderate oven (350 degrees F.) for about 1 hour. Pour off excess fat. Prepare stuffing as follows:

Combine fruit, sugar, bread crumbs, salt, pepper, sage, thyme, and orange juice. Mix well. Stuff ducks lightly, allowing room for the dressing to expand. Sew or lace openings and tie leg ends together so there will be about 3 inches between the legs. Arrange on rack as before. Roast in a moderate oven about ½ hour. Then pour wine over the ducks. Baste at 15-minute intervals with the wine and juices left in bottom of pan. Roast 1 hour longer. Allow approximately 30 to 35 minutes per pound, or a total of about 2½ hours' baking time. Serve with sauce prepared as follows:

Pour off excess fat from juices left in pan. Add ½ cup wine and ½ cup tomato paste. Simmer 5 minutes. Strain raw duck livers through sieve. Pour hot sauce over livers. Cook 1 minute. Season to taste with salt, pepper, and sugar.

ROAST DUCK, SAUTERNE (*Serves 10 to 12*)

2 6-lb. ducks
Salt
2 cups celery, chopped fine
2 cups apples, chopped
3 cups bread crumbs, toasted
2 tbsps. sugar
Grated rind of 2 oranges
1 tsp. salt
¼ tsp. pepper
½ tsp. thyme, marjoram, or sage
½ cup orange juice
2 cups Sauterne or Rhine Wine

Singe, clean, wash, and dry ducks. Rub inside with salt and fill with the following fruit stuffing: Combine celery, apples, and bread crumbs. Add the sugar, grated orange rind, salt, pepper, and thyme, marjoram or sage. Mix well. Moisten dressing with ¼ cup orange juice and ¼ cup wine. Close neck and body cavities with skewers or sew with coarse white thread. Place ducks breast side up on roasting rack in an open pan, and roast in a moderate oven (350 degrees F.), allowing 20 to 25 minutes per pound. Baste several times with mixture of remaining orange juice and wine and with drippings from the bottom of pan.

ROAST GOOSE, CLARET (*Serves 8 to 10*)

1 10-lb. goose
1 lb. prunes
2 lbs. cooking apples, peeled and sliced fine
2 cups Claret or Burgundy
1 cup hot water
1 cup crushed Zwieback
⅓ cup sugar
Salt, pepper, and flour

Singe, clean, wash, and dry goose. Rub inside and outside with salt. Fill goose loosely with fruit stuffing made as follows: Soak prunes in water overnight. Cook until tender in 1 cup wine. Add apples, Zwieback crumbs, sugar, and salt to taste.

After filling goose, close openings with skewers. Tuck under tips of wings and tie legs together. Prick skin at several places to allow fat to run out. Roast breast side down in covered roasting pan in a 400-degree F. oven for 1 hour. Roast breast side up, uncovered, in a 325-degree F. oven until done. Baste frequently with mixture of 1 cup of hot wine and 1 cup of hot water. Allow 20 to 25 minutes per pound for total roasting.

Skim fat from liquid in bottom of pan. Measure liquid, and add enough water to make 3 cups. Thicken with flour as desired. Season with salt and pepper.

RABBIT IN CASSEROLE (*Serves 6*)

- 1 rabbit
- 3 tbsps. flour
- 1 tsp. salt
- ½ tsp. pepper
- 2 tbsps. butter or margarine
- 2 tbsps. cooking oil
- 1 cup Claret or Burgundy
- ½ cup canned or diced fresh tomato
- ½ cup diced celery
- 3 tbsps. sugar

Disjoint the rabbit and shake in paper bag with flour, salt, and pepper. Brown in butter or margarine and oil in skillet. Remove to casserole. Pour wine into skillet, stir well, then pour over rabbit. Add remaining ingredients, cover, and bake in a slow oven (325 degrees F.) for 1 hour.

VENISON

Venison may be broiled, fried, stewed, or roasted, depending upon the cut and the age of the animal. If you're frying or broiling, it is well to do this quickly, for slow cooking toughens the meat. Reduce the cooking time allowed for ordinary meats, as venison is served slightly more rare.

Wine Marinade for Venison

In the preparation of venison, wine marinating is almost essential, as the marinating prevents drying, helps to tenderize this tough-textured meat, and aids in balancing the gamy odors.

Any of the red table wines, such as Claret or Burgundy, may be used to marinate venison. Prepare the marinade by combining one-third vinegar with two-thirds wine. Add one large onion, finely chopped, chopped celery, salt and pepper to taste, and a couple of crushed bay leaves. Bring marinade to a boil and, while warm, pour over meat stored in a crock. Cover, and let stand in the refrigerator, turning the meat occasionally.

Large cuts, such as a haunch, are best if marinated from 10 to 48 hours, and never less than overnight.

When ready to cook, be sure to save the marinade liquid.

POT ROAST OF VENISON

Drain marinated meat well. Dust with flour, and sear in a pan, using 2 to 4 tablespoons shortening. When seared on all sides, strain the marinating liquor and pour over roast. Cover kettle, and let meat simmer until tender. When meat is done, remove, and thicken remaining liquid with flour. Stir in 1 cup of sour cream immediately before serving.

RAGOUT OF VENISON

This recipe calls for 2 pounds of venison meat, marinated as above.

Place the meat in a large saucepan with 4 tablespoons hot fat. Sauté the marinated meat over a hot fire, turning on all sides until well browned. This will take about 5 minutes. Add 1 onion, finely chopped, a pinch of thyme, 1 bay leaf, ½ teaspoon freshly ground black pepper, 1 teaspoon salt, and 1 tablespoon finely chopped bacon.

Add the wine in which the meat was marinated. Cover saucepan, and let cook for about 1 hour over a low flame. If more liquid is needed at this point, add beef stock. Then add one dozen very small white onions, and continue cooking for another hour.

Sauté 12 to 15 medium-sized mushrooms in butter, turning frequently until nicely browned.

Serve ragout on large, hot platter garnished with sautéed mushrooms. Sprinkle finely chopped parsley over all.

ROASTING TENDER CUTS OF VENISON

Marinate saddle, ribs, and loins with wine as described above. Dry well and rub with fat. Roast at 325 degrees F. until tender—2 hours or more. Serve with sauce made as follows:

Strain 2 to 3 cups of the wine marinating liquor, and bring to a boil. Melt a small (4-oz.) glass of currant jelly, add to wine marinating liquor. Thicken to consistency of heavy cream with flour, salt, and pepper to taste. Simmer 10 to 15 minutes.

VENISON STEAKS

Frying and broiling are the easiest and most delicious ways to cook tender cuts from the loin, rib chops, or ham. Pound the steaks slightly with a meat hammer or blunt tool, brush with oil, and proceed as you would with beef. Take care not to overcook, as this tends to toughen and dry the meat. Serve with wine sauce.

Wine Sauce for Venison Steaks

To ½ cup Sherry or Port wine add 1 tablespoon currant jelly and spread on steaks after they are well seared in fat.

CHAPTER 11

FRUITS, DESSERTS, AND DESSERT SAUCES

Wine which Music is—
Music and Wine are one.

RALPH WALDO EMERSON

In the world of fruits and desserts, wine offers a sparkling array of flavor accents from which to choose. Any of the red and white table wines may be used, as well as Sherry and the dessert wines, such as Port, Muscatel, and Tokay.

With fresh, canned, or frozen fruits, simply pour some of your table wine over the fruit, chill in the refrigerator, and serve. Peaches, pears, and grapes combine well with Sauterne and Rhine Wine; mixed fruits or melons blend well with either the red or white table wines. When the red or white table wines are added, fruits may be lightly sugared, if desired.

In fruit gelatin desserts the table wines, both red and white, are a good choice; Port, Muscatel, Tokay, and Sherry are equally interesting and delightful.

WINE APPLE PUDDING (*Serves 6*)

4 tart apples, sliced
2 tbsps. lemon juice
⅔ cup Port or Muscatel
⅓ cup sugar
2 eggs, beaten
¼ tsp. salt
¼ tsp. nutmeg
½ tsp. cinnamon
2 cups dry bread crumbs
⅓ cup butter or margarine

Pour lemon juice and wine over sliced apples and let stand. Cream together butter or margarine and sugar. Add beaten eggs, salt, and spices. Combine with the apples and the wine. Turn into baking dish, cover, and bake in a moderate oven (350 degrees F.) for 35 or 40 minutes. Serve, while still warm, with Fluffy Wine Sauce.

Fluffy Wine Sauce

- 2 tbsps. butter or margarine
- ¾ cup confectioner's sugar
- 3 tbsps. Port or Muscatel
- 2 tsps. grated lemon rind

Cream butter or margarine until light and fluffy. Blend in sugar. Add wine, and beat until mixture is smooth. Add lemon rind.

APPLE TARTLETS (*Makes 6 tarts*)

- 5 apples
- ½ cup Port or Muscatel
- ¾ cup sugar
- ½ tsp. mace
- ½ tsp. cinnamon
- 1 tsp. grated lemon rind
- 6 baked tart shells
- 6 baked toppings for tart shells

Pare the apples and cut in eighths. Add the wine (and ¼ cup water if the apples are not very juicy), and cook slowly in a covered kettle for 20 to 30 minutes, or until soft. Stir to prevent sticking. Add the sugar, and cook long enough to dissolve sugar. Add spices and lemon rind. Fill warm tart shells with warm applesauce. Top with baked pastry topping. Sprinkle with a dash of cinnamon or mace. Serve warm.

BAKED APPLES WITH PORT (*Serves 4*)

4 large baking apples
⅓ cup sugar
½ cup boiling water
½ cup Port wine

Wash and core the apples. Peel upper ⅓ of each. Place in casserole. Dissolve sugar in water. Pour over apples. Cover, and bake in a moderate oven (375 degrees F.) for 30 to 40 minutes. Remove apples to serving dishes. Pour 2 tablespoons Port wine into each apple. Boil down remaining syrup until fairly thick, and pour over apples to glaze them.

APPLE FRITTERS, TOKAY (*Serves 6 to 8*)

4 to 6 cooking apples
½ cup granulated sugar
½ cup and 2 tbsps. Tokay, Muscatel, or Port
1 tsp. grated lemon rind
1 cup flour
½ tsp. salt
2 eggs, beaten separately
½ cup water
2 tbsps. butter, melted
Fat for frying
Powdered sugar
Cinnamon

Peel and core apples. Remove a slice from both the stem and the blossom end. Slice the remainder of the apples in slices about ⅛ inch thick. Place in shallow bowl. Cover with ½ cup wine, granulated sugar, and grated lemon rind. Let stand for 2 or 3 hours.

Make a fritter batter as follows: Sift together the flour and salt. Add water and melted butter and remaining 2 tablespoons wine to the lightly beaten egg yolks. Add liquid mixture to flour and salt, and beat until smooth, then fold in the stiffly beaten egg whites.

Dip the apple slices in the batter, and fry in deep fat

at 370 degrees F. for approximately 2 minutes. (The fat has reached the right temperature for fritter frying when an inch cube of bread browns in 50 seconds.)

Drain the fritters and sprinkle with powdered sugar. Serve with whipped cream sweetened with powdered sugar, flavored with wine, and sprinkled with cinnamon.

DEEP DISH APPLE PIE, TOKAY

(*Yield: 6 individual pies*)

Pastry

1¼ cups sifted flour
½ tsp. salt
⅓ cup shortening
2 tbsps. cold water

Mix and sift flour and salt. Cut in shortening until mixture is the consistency of coarse corn meal. Add water in small amounts. Toss dry ingredients with water lightly until dough holds together. Wrap dough in waxed paper. Chill thoroughly. Roll, and cut into ½-inch strips for lattice pastry.

Pie Filling

3 cups sliced apples
¾ cup sugar
½ tsp. salt
½ tsp. cinnamon
⅛ tsp. nutmeg
2 tbsps. flour
2 tbsps. butter or margarine
2 tbsps. lemon juice
¾ cup Tokay (Port or Muscatel may also be used in this recipe)

Arrange a layer of sliced apples in each individual deep-dish pie shell. Mix sugar, salt, spices, and flour. Sprinkle half the dry ingredients over the layers of apples. Add remaining apples and remaining dry ingredients in succeeding layers. Dot with butter or margarine. Sprinkle with lemon juice. Add 2 tablespoons wine to each pie. Top with lattice pastry. Bake in hot oven (450 degrees F.) for 10 minutes, then reduce heat to moderate (350 degrees F.), and bake 30 to 35 minutes longer, until the apples are done and the crust is browned.

BANANAS IN CLARET (*Serves 4*)

4 small bananas, green tipped
2 tbsps. butter or margarine
Few grains salt
1 cup Claret or Burgundy
1 cup sugar
1 tbsp. cornstarch
Dash of nutmeg

Peel whole bananas and lightly brown in butter or margarine. Heat wine. Add sugar mixed with cornstarch, and cook, stirring, until clear and slightly thickened. Add nutmeg and salt, and pour over bananas. Simmer slowly for 15 minutes.

BLUEBERRY TARTS, MUSCATEL (*Makes 8 tarts*)

3 cups fresh blueberries
6 tbsps. sugar
½ cup Muscatel
¼ cup cornstarch
½ tsp. salt
1 tbsp. lemon juice
Tart shells

Combine blueberries, Muscatel, and lemon juice. Mix cornstarch and sugar and add to mixture. Cook in double boiler until thickened. Cool slightly. Pour into tart shells. Cool, and garnish with whipped cream.

BROILED GRAPEFRUIT, SHERRY (*Serves 6*)

3 grapefruit
6 tbsps. Sherry
3 tbsps. light brown sugar
3 tsps. butter or margarine

Halve grapefruit. Cut around core with scissors and remove. Loosen each section by cutting around it with a sharp knife. Pour 1 tablespoon Sherry on each half and let stand ½ hour. Sprinkle halves with brown sugar and dot with butter. Place under the broiler for 10 minutes, or until warmed through and lightly browned around the edges. Serve at once.

WINE FRUIT COMPOTE (*Serves 6*)

- 1 cup sugar
- 1½ cups water
- 4 to 6 fresh peaches, sliced
- 8 apricots, halved
- 1½ cups logan or blackberries
- 6 tbsps. Port, Muscatel, or Tokay

Boil sugar and water for 3 minutes. Cook peaches and apricots lightly in the syrup for 3 to 5 minutes. Remove to refrigerator dish. Add the berries to the syrup, and simmer 3 minutes. Cool. Add to peaches and apricots. Add wine to syrup, and pour over fruit. Chill thoroughly. Serve in glass dessert dishes.

SHERRY FRUIT CUP (*Serves 8*)

- 2 pears, cut in cubes
- 1 cup grapes, seeds removed
- 1 cup orange sections
- Mint, if desired
- 1 cup melon balls, or
- 1 cup bananas, sliced
- Lemon or lime juice
- ½ cup Sherry

Arrange fruit in sherbet or cocktail glasses. Sprinkle with lemon or lime juice. Pour 1 tablespoon Sherry into each dish. Chill one hour. Serve garnished with a sprig of mint.

WINE BAKED ORANGES (*Serves 8*)

8 oranges or tangerines
1 cup Claret or Burgundy

Cut peeling of fruit into six sections, cutting down about 1½ inches. Turn petal-like sections of peeling under, removing part of the white membrane. Place on baking dish. Pour wine into each piece of fruit and bake in a 400-degree F. oven for about 10 minutes.

SPICED PEARS (*Serves 8*)

4 pears, peeled, halved, and cored
2 cups Sauterne or Rhine Wine
1 cup water
1 cup sugar
1 inch stick cinnamon
1 piece ginger root
6 whole cloves

Combine wine, water, sugar, and spices, and cook for 5 minutes. Add the pears, and simmer very slowly until tender.

WINE BAKED PEARS (*Serves 6*)

6 firm pears
½ cup honey
½ cup cake crumbs
1 cup Port, Muscatel, or Tokay
3 tbsps. chopped pecans
1 tbsp. lemon peel, grated
1 cup sour cream
Grated cinnamon or mace

Cut pears in half lengthwise. Remove core. Arrange in baking dish. Prepare filling by combining 2 tablespoons honey with the cake crumbs. Add 2 tablespoons wine, the nuts, and the grated lemon peel. Fill core cavities with mixture. Top with matching pear half. Pour remaining wine over the pears. Bake in a moderate oven (350 degrees F.) for about 10 minutes. Remove from oven. Drip 1 teaspoon honey over each pear. Return to oven, and bake until done—5 to 10 minutes. Serve with wine syrup. If desired, top with sour cream which has been sweetened with remaining ¼ cup honey. Top sour cream with dash of grated cinnamon or mace.

PEACH WINE JELLY (*Serves 6 to 8*)

- 2 tbsps. unflavored gelatin
- ½ cup cold water
- ¾ cup boiling water
- ¾ cup hot peach juice
- 2 tbsps. lemon juice
- ¾ cup sugar
- ½ cup orange juice
- 1¼ cups Port or Muscatel

Soften gelatin in cold water. Dissolve in hot water or hot water and peach juice. Add lemon juice, sugar, and orange juice. Cool, and add the wine. Pour into mold that has been rinsed in cold water, and chill until firm. Serve with sliced peaches marinated in wine.

HONEY-WINE PICKLED FRUITS (*Serves 12 to 16*)

- 1 cup honey
- ¾ cup vinegar
- 10 whole cloves
- 3 inches stick cinnamon
- ¾ cup Port or Muscatel
- 1½ qts. fresh or drained canned fruits

Simmer honey, vinegar, and spices for 5 minutes. Add wine and prepared fruits, and simmer 15 minutes, or until fresh fruits are tender. Cool; store in refrigerator.

Apple quarters or peach, pear, or apricot halves, or a mixture of fruits, may be used.

WINE POTPOURRI (*Serves 4 to 6*)

1 lb. dried fruits—prunes, pears, peaches, and apricots
¼ lb. sugar
Claret or Burgundy
1 stick cinnamon
Peel of 1 lemon, cut in thin strips

Soak the dried fruits in wine overnight. Place fruits in saucepan with enough wine to cover. Add ¼ cup sugar, cinnamon stick, and lemon peel. Cook slowly, covered. When fruits are tender, remove from the sauce. Continue cooking wine mixture until it is syrupy. Chill fruits and wine mixture and serve very cold with heavy cream, plain or whipped.

CLARET PRUNES (*Serves 4 to 6*)

1 lb. prunes
¾ cup sugar
1 lemon, sliced
Stick cinnamon
1 cup Claret or Burgundy

Soak prunes in water overnight. Add sugar, sliced lemon, and stick cinnamon. Simmer slowly until prunes are almost tender. Add wine, and simmer 15 minutes longer.

SHERRY PRUNE WHIP (*Serves 6*)

1½ cups prune pulp
½ cup Sherry
2 egg whites, beaten until stiff
1 cup whipping cream, whipped

Mix Sherry with prune pulp. Fold in the stiffly beaten egg whites and the whipped cream. Serve piled high in sherbet dishes.

PRUNE PORT WINE WHIP (*Serves 6 to 8*)

2 tbsps. gelatin
⅓ cup cold water
2 cups hot prune pulp
½ cup Port
Walnuts for garnish
2 tbsps. lemon juice
⅓ cup sugar or honey
1 cup whipping cream, whipped

Soak gelatin in cold water. Dissolve in hot prune pulp. Add the wine, lemon juice, and sugar or honey. Allow to cool. When mixture begins to thicken, whip the cream and fold into prune-whip mixture. Turn into mold which has been rinsed in cold water. Chill until firm. Unmold, and serve with whipped cream garnished with walnuts

RAISIN PORT PIE (*One 9-inch pie*)

2 cups raisins
¾ cup Port
¼ cup lemon juice
Butter
Rind of one lemon, cut in fine strips
2 tbsps. cornstarch

Wash the raisins. Soak in warm water about 2 hours. Cook slowly until plump. Drain. Cover with the Port wine and marinate for 1 hour. Blend cornstarch with lemon juice and mix through raisins. Add strips of lemon peel. Pour into pastry-lined pie pan, dot with butter, and cover with lattice strips of pastry. Bake in a 450-degree F. oven for 10 minutes. Then reduce heat to 350 degrees and bake ½ hour longer.

CLARET RASPBERRY FLOAT (*Serves 4*)

1 pint raspberry sherbet
2 cups Claret or Burgundy
Berries for garnishing
1 cup raspberry syrup
Sparkling water

Chill the wine, syrup, and sparkling water. Pour ½ cup wine in each glass; add ¼ cup raspberry syrup. Mix well. Add sparkling water to fill glass to 1 inch from brim. Top with a scoop of raspberry sherbet. Garnish with fresh berries. Serve with parfait spoons and straws.

RASPBERRY CHARLOTTE (*Serves 6 to 8*)

1½ cups milk
1 tbsp. gelatin
¼ cup Port or Muscatel
3 eggs, separated
½ cup sugar
⅛ tsp. salt
1 cup stale sponge cake crumbs
1 pint fresh raspberries
1 cup water
1½ tbsps. cornstarch
½ cup sugar
⅛ tsp. salt
1 tbsp. lemon juice
½ cup Port or Muscatel

Scald milk. Soften gelatin in ¼ cup wine. Beat egg yolks with sugar. Stir a little hot milk into the egg mixture, then add egg mixture to hot milk slowly, stirring all the while. Cook, stirring constantly, over low flame (or over hot water) until custard coats the spoon. Remove from heat, and stir in softened gelatin. Cool. Add salt to egg whites. Beat until stiff, and fold into custard mixture. Place cake crumbs in the bottom of a 1-quart mold. Pour in custard mixture. Chill until firm. When ready to serve, unmold, and pour raspberry sauce over mold.

To make the sauce, cook 1 cup raspberries and water

10 minutes. Rub through strainer to remove seeds. Mix together cornstarch, sugar, and ⅛ tsp. salt. Stir into raspberry juice, and cook until mixture thickens and becomes clear, stirring constantly. Add lemon juice, ½ cup wine, and remaining raspberries. More sugar may be added if desired. Chill sauce before serving.

RASPBERRY PORT WINE JELLY (*Serves 4 to 6*)

- 1 tbsp and 1 tsp. plain gelatin
- ⅓ cup cold water
- ½ cup boiling water
- ¾ cup raspberry juice
- ⅓ cup sugar
- ½ tsp. salt
- 2 tbsps. lemon juice
- ¾ cup Port

Soak gelatin in cold water. Dissolve in boiling water. Add raspberry juice, sugar, and salt. Heat over double boiler if gelatin is not thoroughly dissolved. Cool. Add lemon juice and Port. Pour into mold which has been rinsed with cold water. Chill until firm. Unmold, and serve with fresh fruits.

CALIFORNIA SQUASH PIE (*One 9-inch pie*)

- 2 cups cooked, mashed squash or pumpkin
- 3 eggs, beaten slightly
- ¾ cup granulated sugar
- 1 tsp. salt
- 1 tsp. cinnamon
- ½ tsp. nutmeg
- ⅛ tsp. cloves
- 1½ cups milk, scalded
- ½ cup Port or Muscatel

Add sugar and seasonings to beaten eggs, then add scalded milk slowly. Add wine to squash or pumpkin, then add to custard mixture. Pour into pastry-lined pie pan. Bake in a 450-degree F. oven for 10 minutes, then reduce heat to 350 degrees F. and bake 30 minutes longer. Serve with whipped cream if desired.

SHERRIED SWEET POTATO PIE (*Serves 5 to 6*)

- 1½ cups mashed sweet potato
- 2 eggs, beaten slightly
- ⅓ cup brown or granulated sugar
- ¾ tsp. salt
- ½ tsp. cinnamon
- ¼ tsp. ginger
- ¼ tsp. allspice
- 1 tsp. grated orange rind
- ½ cup milk
- ¼ cup Sherry
- 2 tbsps. melted butter

Add slightly beaten eggs to mashed sweet potato. Add sugar, salt, cinnamon, ginger, allspice, and grated orange rind. Add milk, Sherry, and melted butter. Pour into pastry-lined 8-inch pie pan. Sprinkle with nutmeg. Bake in hot oven (450 degrees F.) for 10 minutes, then reduce heat to moderate (350 degrees F.), and bake 25 to 35 minutes longer, or until firm when tested with a knife.

STRAWBERRY SHORTCAKE, GOURMET (*Serves 6 to 8*)

- 1¾ cups milk
- 3 eggs
- ⅛ tsp. salt
- ½ cup sugar
- 1¼ cups Port, Muscatel, or Tokay
- 1 pt. fresh strawberries, sliced
- 1 9-inch sponge cake layer

Scald the milk. Beat eggs until light. Add salt and 3 tablespoons sugar to the eggs. Pour scalded milk into egg mixture, stirring all the while. Cook over boiling water, stirring constantly, until custard coats the spoon. Stir in ¼ cup wine. Combine remaining sugar and wine with strawberries.

Split sponge cake and arrange strawberries between layers and on top just before serving. Pour some of the strawberry juice and wine over the cake. May be topped with whipped cream or wine-flavored custard sauce.

STRAWBERRY BLANCMANGE (*Serves 6*)

3 tbsps. cornstarch
¼ tsp. salt
¼ cup sugar
½ cup cold milk
1¼ cups scalded milk
1¼ cups Muscatel or Port
1 pint strawberries

Mix cornstarch, salt, and sugar with cold milk. Add the scalded milk, and cook the mixture over hot water until it thickens. Add ¼ cup of the wine. Pour into mold which has been rinsed in cold water. Chill until firm. Pour remaining 1 cup of wine over strawberries and allow berries to stand in the wine for ½ hour in a cool place. Unmold the blancmange, and serve strawberries in wine around the mold.

PINEAPPLE-STRAWBERRY FRUIT CUP, RED WINE (*Serves 4 to 6*)

1 medium-sized pineapple
1 pt. fresh strawberries
½ cup sugar
1 cup Claret or Burgundy

Split pineapple straight through the center. Cut out most of the pulp, leaving a basketlike shell. Cut pulp into cubes. Slice the strawberries. Mix strawberries and pineapple. Add sugar. Fill fruit into pineapple halves. Pour wine over fruit. Serve from fruit basket into punch cups or sherbet glasses.

If this fruit cup is to be served as the appetizer course, sugar may be omitted.

STRAWBERRIES, SAUTERNE (*Serves 6*)

1 qt. strawberries
1 cup confectioner's sugar
1 cup Sauterne or Rhine Wine

Wash and hull the berries. Arrange in refrigerator bowl. Pour wine over berries. Chill at least 1 hour. Sprinkle with confectioner's sugar and serve.

STRAWBERRY PIE À LA PORT

1 baked pie shell
1 qt. strawberries
1 cup sugar
½ cup and 2 tbsps. Port
2 tbsps. lemon juice
1 tbsp. and 1 tsp. unflavored gelatin
⅓ cup cold water
½ pint whipping cream
3 tbsps. confectioner's sugar

Wash and hull strawberries. Reserve a few for garnishing. Slice remaining berries. Add the sugar, ½ cup of the wine, and the lemon juice, and set in refrigerator for about 15 minutes. Soak gelatin in cold water. Drain juice from berries, add to gelatin, and heat in top of double boiler until gelatin is dissolved. Cool. When mixture begins to congeal, add the strawberries. Pour into pie shell. Chill. Serve topped with whipped cream to which remaining 2 tablespoons of Port and the confectioner's sugar have been added.

FRUIT WINE SHORTCAKE

Baking-powder biscuit layers
Peaches or apricots
Sauterne or Rhine Wine
Sugar
Cream

Bake shortcake according to favorite recipe. Bake in two layers. Peel peaches or apricots and pour wine over fruit to cover. Sprinkle generously with sugar. Let fruit stand in wine for 1 hour. Remove fruit, and cook the juice until it forms a thin syrup. Cool. Arrange fruit on layers of shortcake. Pour syrup over fruit. Garnish with whipped cream, almonds, or berries.

BAKED ALASKA (*Serves 1*)

Dip a slice of pineapple in Sherry and place on top of a slice of pound or sponge cake. Top this with a generous scoop of ice cream, cover with meringue, and place in a hot oven (450 degrees F.) for 5 minutes. Serve immediately.

SHERRY CHIFFON PIE

1 tbsp. plain gelatin
¼ cup cold water
1½ cups hot milk
2 eggs, separated
6 tbsps. sugar
½ tsp. almond extract
¼ cup Sherry
Few grains salt
1 baked 9-inch pie shell
Powdered nutmeg

Add gelatin to cold water and let stand. Beat egg yolks with 2 tbsps. sugar, stir into hot milk, and cook, stirring, until mixture coats a metal spoon. Remove from heat, add almond extract, Sherry, and softened gelatin, and stir until dissolved. Cool until slightly thickened. Add salt to egg whites, beat stiff; gradually beat in remaining 4 tbsps. sugar. Fold into gelatin mixture, blending thoroughly. Pour into a baked pie shell or graham-cracker crust. Sprinkle top lightly with nutmeg. Chill until firm.

CALIFORNIA SYLLABUB (*Serves 4*)

½ pint whipping cream
Grated rind of 1 lemon
½ cup Port or Muscatel
Ladyfingers

Whip the cream. Add grated lemon rind. Stir the wine into the cream mixture gradually. Serve heaped in sherbet glasses which have been lined with ladyfingers.

CRÊPES SUZETTE, PORT SAUCE
(*Yield: 2½ doz. small cakes*)

1¾ cups flour, sifted
⅓ cup powdered sugar
¼ tsp. salt
1 cup milk
1 tsp. lemon rind, grated
3 eggs, beaten
½ cup Port or Muscatel
¼ cup butter or margarine, melted

Mix and sift dry ingredients. Stir in milk. Add beaten eggs, ¼ cup wine, the melted butter or margarine, and the grated lemon rind. Beat until smooth. Grease the pan with butter or margarine. Heat pan. Make very thin pancakes about 4 inches in diameter; cook cakes until lightly browned. Sprinkle with powdered sugar and remaining wine; roll. Keep hot until ready to serve.

Port Sauce

½ cup sugar
2 tsps. cornstarch
¼ tsp. salt
¼ tsp. mace
½ cup cold water
1 tbsp. lemon juice
½ tsp. lemon rind
1 cup Port or Muscatel

Mix sugar, cornstarch, salt, and mace. Add cold water, lemon juice, and the lemon rind. Cook until thickened and clear, stirring constantly. Add the wine, and cook 1 minute longer. Serve hot with Crêpes Suzette, or any bland-flavored dessert.

SHERRY TAPIOCA CREAM (*Serves 4*)

⅓ cup quick-cooking tapioca	2 eggs, separated
⅛ tsp. salt	3 cups rich milk
¼ cup sugar	1 cup Sherry
	Whipped cream
	Cherries for garnish

Combine tapioca, sugar, and salt. Add the egg yolks which have been beaten slightly. Scald the milk, and add 1 cup scalded milk to the tapioca mixture. Add remaining milk, and cook over hot water until mixture thickens. Add the Sherry, and cook 2 minutes longer. Remove from over hot water. Fold small amount of hot mixture into stiffly beaten egg whites. Mix with remaining hot mixture. Turn into dish to cool. Chill. Serve piled high in sherbet glasses garnished with whipped cream and maraschino cherries.

NOTE: *If pearl tapioca is used, double the amount of tapioca, soak in cold water for 1 hour, and cook longer —until the pearls are clear.*

SPANISH CREAM (*Serves 4 to 6*)

2 tbsps. unflavored gelatin	½ cup sugar
1¾ cups milk	¼ tsp. salt
3 eggs, separated	¼ cup Sherry

Soak gelatin in ½ cup cold milk. Scald remaining milk. Beat egg yolks until light. Add gelatin and sugar to egg yolks. Pour scalded milk into the egg-yolk mixture slowly. Mix well, and add the salt. Cook over hot water, stirring constantly, until the custard thickens. Cool slightly, and add the Sherry. Chill until mixture just begins to congeal. Beat egg whites until stiff. Fold custard mixture into whites. Pour into mold that has been rinsed in cold water. Chill until firm.

SHERRY CREAM (*Serves 6 to 8*)

1 tbsp. gelatin
½ cup cold water
½ cup boiling water
2 tbsps. lemon juice
½ cup sugar
½ cup Sherry
1 cup evaporated milk

Soften gelatin in cold water. Add boiling water and stir until completely dissolved. Stir in the sugar. Add Sherry. Chill milk thoroughly. When Sherry mixture begins to jell, whip milk until stiff. Fold in the lemon juice, then the jelly. Pour into a mold to set or pile into serving dishes and chill.

SHERRY CUSTARD (*Serves 4*)

2 egg yolks
¼ cup sugar
¼ tsp. salt
1¼ cups milk
¼ cup Sherry
Dash of nutmeg

Combine egg yolks, sugar, and salt in top of double boiler. Add the milk, and cook over hot water, stirring constantly, until mixture coats the spoon. Cool, and add the Sherry. Top with a dusting of nutmeg.

SHERRY MALLOBET (*Serves 4*)

24 marshmallows
¼ cup Sherry
¼ cup cold water
2 tbsps. lemon juice
2 tbsps. sugar
¼ cup egg whites (about 2 eggs)
Few grains salt

Add cold water to marshmallows and melt over hot water. Stir frequently. Add Sherry, lemon juice, and 1 tablespoon sugar. Freeze to a mush. Stir well. Add remaining sugar and salt to egg whites. Whip stiff. Combine, and freeze to a mush. Stir thoroughly, and finish freezing.

SHERRY FLUMMERY (*Serves 6*)

2 tbsps. gelatin
1 can evaporated milk
1½ cups water
3 eggs, separated
½ cup sugar
½ tsp. salt
⅓ cup Sherry
3 tbsps. lemon juice
1 tsp. grated lemon rind
1 cup applesauce, sweetened, strained

Soak gelatin in ½ cup cold water. Scald the evaporated milk and ½ cup water. Beat egg yolks with sugar and salt. Add remaining ½ cup water. Stir into hot liquid. Cook over hot water until mixture is smooth and clings to spoon. Dissolve gelatin in hot custard mixture. Cool. Add the Sherry, lemon juice, lemon rind, and the applesauce. Chill until mixture begins to thicken. Beat with rotary beater. Beat egg whites until stiff. Fold into mixture. Turn into mold which has been rinsed in cold water. Chill until firm. Unmold, and serve with Sherry Strawberry Sauce.

Sherry Strawberry Sauce

1 pt. strawberries, fresh or frozen
1½ tbsps. cornstarch
½ cup sugar
1 cup water
¼ tsp. salt
1 tbsp. lemon juice
3 tbsps. Sherry

Cook one cup of the strawberries and the water for 5 minutes. Rub through strainer. Mix together cornstarch, sugar, and salt. Stir into strawberry juice, and cook until mixture thickens and becomes clear. Stir constantly while cooking. Add lemon juice and Sherry. Cool slightly. Add the remaining strawberries.

SHERRY EGGNOG PIE

(Makes filling for one 9-inch pie)

1 baked pie shell
1 tbsp. and 1 tsp. unflavored gelatin
¼ cup cold water
3 eggs, separated
½ cup sugar
1 cup top milk, scalded
½ tsp. salt
¼ cup Sherry
½ tsp. vanilla
½ tsp. grated nutmeg

Soften gelatin in cold water. Beat egg yolks until light and creamy. Add ¼ cup sugar and mix well, then add the scalded milk slowly, and the salt. Cook over boiling water for 5 minutes, stirring constantly. Add softened gelatin. Stir until dissolved. Cool. Add the Sherry and vanilla. Chill until mixture congeals slightly. Beat egg whites until stiff. Fold in remaining sugar, then fold in slightly stiffened gelatin mixture. Pour into baked pie shell. Sprinkle with grated nutmeg. Chill until firm.

SHERRY MACAROON MOUSSE

(Makes 1 quart)

2 tsps. unflavored gelatin
¼ cup cold water
1 cup light cream
½ cup sugar
12 macaroons, crumbled
½ tsp. salt
½ cup Sherry
½ pint whipping cream, whipped

Soak gelatin in cold water. Dissolve over hot water and add cream. Add sugar and salt. Chill until gelatin begins to congeal. Stir in the Sherry and fold in the whipped cream. Freeze in refrigerator freezing tray, with regulator turned to coldest point, until mixture is about half frozen, then beat with a rotary beater until mixture is smooth. Add the crumbled macaroons, and return to freezing tray. Freeze until firm.

CHOCOLATE SPONGE LOGS (*Serves 6*)

⅓ cup cake flour	½ tsp. salt
3 tbsps. cocoa	3 eggs, separated
½ tsp. baking powder	¾ cup powdered sugar
2 tsps. Sherry	

Sift together flour, cocoa, baking powder, and salt. Beat egg yolks until thick. Stir in the powdered sugar gradually. Add half the flour mixture. Stir in the Sherry. Finally fold in the stiffly beaten egg whites. Pour into a shallow pan about 10 x 14 inches which has been greased, lined with wax paper, greased again, and floured. Bake in a moderate oven (350 degrees F.) for 12 or 13 minutes. Invert pan on cloth. Remove paper from bottom of cake. Allow to cool. For logs, cut into six pieces, spread with Orange Sherry Filling, and roll individually. Otherwise, spread the entire sheet with filling and make one large roll.

Orange Sherry Filling

½ cup sugar	¼ cup Sherry
2½ tbsps. cornstarch	1 tbsp. lemon juice
¼ tsp. salt	1 tsp. grated orange rind
1 egg yolk, slightly beaten	1 tbsp. butter or margarine
½ cup orange juice	
¼ cup water	

Combine sugar, cornstarch, and salt. Add egg yolk, orange juice, and water. Cook over boiling water for 5 minutes. Add the Sherry and lemon juice, and cook 10 minutes, stirring occasionally. Add orange rind and the butter or margarine. Cool before spreading on cake.

SHERRY LEMON SOUFFLÉ (*Serves 6*)

¼ cup butter or margarine
6 tbsps. flour
¾ cup milk
½ cup sugar
½ tsp. salt
½ cup Sherry
¼ cup lemon juice
Grated rind of 2 lemons
6 eggs, separated
Powdered sugar

Blend flour with softened butter or margarine. Heat the milk and add to the flour-butter mixture slowly. Add the sugar and salt. Cook slowly, stirring constantly, until sauce begins to thicken. Stir in the Sherry, and continue cooking and stirring until smooth and very thick. Add the lemon juice and the grated lemon rind. Cool mixture slightly. Beat egg yolks until light and blend with sauce. Fold in the stiffly beaten egg whites, carefully retaining as much of the air as possible. Pour into buttered baking dish. Sprinkle with powdered sugar run through flour sieve. Bake in a moderately slow oven (325 degrees F.) for 1 hour. Serve with Sherry Lemon Sauce.

Sherry Lemon Sauce (*Yield: sauce for 6 servings*)

1 tbsp. cornstarch
½ tsp. salt
⅓ cup sugar
¾ cup boiling water
¼ cup Sherry
2 tsps. grated lemon rind
2 tsps. lemon juice
1 tbsp. butter or margarine

Blend cornstarch, salt, and sugar. Add boiling water gradually. Cook, stirring constantly, until it begins to thicken. Add the wine, and simmer, stirring until smooth and clear, for about 10 minutes. Add lemon rind and juice. Stir in the butter or margarine.

ZABAGLIONE (*Serves 6 to 8*)

6 eggs
½ tsp. salt
6 tbsps. sugar
1½ cups Sherry
Grated cinnamon or nutmeg

Beat eggs with a rotary beater. Add the salt. Dissolve sugar in Sherry and add to eggs, beating all the while. Place over hot water, and cook very, very slowly, beating or stirring constantly to maintain a smooth consistency. Cook until mixture is as thick as thick cream. Serve hot or cold in tall glasses sprinkled with cinnamon or nutmeg.

Zabaglione may also be used as a rich pudding sauce.

WINE TRIFLE (*Serves 5 to 6*)

1⅔ cups rich milk
4 egg yolks, beaten slightly
¼ cup sugar
¼ tsp. salt
½ tsp. vanilla
⅔ cup Sherry
1 sponge cake, 2 inches thick
⅓ cup raspberry or blackberry jam
⅓ cup toasted almonds, split
Whipped cream

Scald the milk. Combine eggs, sugar, and salt. Add scalded milk to egg mixture, stirring constantly. Turn into top of double boiler. Cook over hot water, stirring constantly, until mixture is thickened and coats the spoon. Cool. Add vanilla and ⅓ cup of the Sherry. Beat with rotary beater. Set custard in refrigerator to chill. Cut sponge cake lengthwise into 2 layers. Spread with jam. Top with second half of cake and spread with remaining jam. Arrange cake in shallow glass dessert dish. Sprinkle remaining ⅓ cup wine over the cake. Let stand while custard is chilling. Pour custard over cake. Garnish with whipped cream topped with split toasted almonds.

BREAD PUDDING WITH WINE SAUCE

(*Serves* 6)

- 4 slices bread, buttered
- 3 cups milk
- 4 eggs
- ¼ cup sugar
- ½ tsp. salt
- ¼ cup Port, Muscatel, or Tokay
- ½ tsp. vanilla

Arrange bread in bottom of buttered baking dish. Scald the milk. Beat eggs. Add sugar and salt. Add milk to egg mixture gradually, then add the wine and the vanilla. Pour custard over bread, and bake in a pan of hot water in a moderate oven (350 degrees F.) for about 40 minutes. Cool.

If desired, top with a meringue made as follows: Beat 2 egg whites with ¼ teaspoon salt until they begin to stiffen. Then add ¼ cup sugar gradually, beating all the while, until mixture stands in peaks. Spread on pudding, and bake in a moderate oven (350 degrees F.) for about 12 minutes, or until lightly browned. Serve with Wine Sauce.

Wine Sauce (*Yield: 1 pint sauce*)

- 2 tbsps. cornstarch
- 4 tbsps. sugar
- 1 cup fruit syrup (left from canned fruit)
- 2 tsps. lemon juice
- Peeling of ¼ lemon, cut in strips
- 1 cup Port, Muscatel, or Tokay

Add sugar to cornstarch. Add fruit syrup gradually, stirring until blended. Add lemon peel, and cook, stirring constantly, until thickened and clear. Add the wine and lemon juice. Bring to a boil. Chill, and serve.

CURRANT JELLY BREAD PUDDING
(*Serves 6*)

3 tbsps. butter or margarine
3¾ cups warm milk
4 eggs
½ cup sugar
6 tbsps. Port or Tokay
2 cups dry bread cubes
3 tbsps. currant jelly

Melt butter in warm milk. Separate two eggs, reserving the whites for meringue. Beat remaining 2 whole eggs and 2 egg yolks with ¼ cup sugar until light. Stir into milk. Add wine and bread cubes. Pour mixture into pudding dish, and bake 30 minutes in moderately hot oven (375 degrees F.). Cool slightly. Spread thinly with jelly.

Beat remaining 2 egg whites until stiff. Add remaining ¼ cup sugar. Spread meringue over top of pudding. Return to oven until meringue is lightly browned.

CHRISTMAS PUDDING (*Serves 10 to 12*)

1 cup chopped suet
1 cup molasses
1 cup sweet milk
1 cup sour cream
1 egg, beaten
2½ cups all-purpose flour
1 tsp. soda
½ tsp. salt
1 tsp. cinnamon
½ tsp. ground cloves
1 cup raisins
1 cup nut meats
¼ cup Port or Muscatel

Combine suet, molasses, sweet milk, sour cream, and beaten egg. Sift together 2 cups flour with soda, salt, cinnamon, and ground cloves. Combine the two mixtures. Stir in raisins and nut-meats which have been mixed with remaining ½ cup flour. Turn into pudding mold or tightly closed pan which has been greased and floured. Place on a rack in a large pan partly filled with water, and steam 2 hours. Unmold the pudding, and pour the wine over it. Serve at once, or wrap in a cloth and store in a cool place until served.

Wine Sauce for Christmas Pudding

¼ cup butter or margarine
¾ cup confectioner's sugar
½ tsp. ground nutmeg
Salt
¼ cup Port or Muscatel

Cream butter or margarine until light and fluffy. Blend in the sugar gradually. Add the wine, and stir until smooth. Add nutmeg and salt to taste. Serve with Christmas Pudding.

STEAMED-DATE-AND-NUT PUDDING
(*Serves 8*)

¾ cup butter or margarine
1½ cups dates, chopped fine
¾ cup chopped nuts
3½ cups soft bread crumbs
3 tsps. baking powder
½ tsp. salt
¾ cup milk
3 eggs
¾ cup sugar
¾ cup Sherry

Cream butter or margarine. Add dates and nuts and mix well. Combine bread crumbs, baking powder, and salt, and stir in the milk. Add to date-nut mixture. Beat eggs. Add sugar, and beat until light. Add to batter. Finally stir in ⅓ cup of the wine. Turn into a 1-quart greased pudding mold. Cover, and steam 2 to 3 hours. Serve with Sherried Whipped Cream.

Sherried Whipped Cream

½ pint whipping cream	3 tbsps. powdered sugar
3 tbsps. Sherry	

Thoroughly chill heavy cream, whipper, and bowl. Beat until cream begins to thicken. Add sugar, and beat until thick. Finally, fold in the Sherry.

FIG NEWTON PUDDING (*Serves 3*)

15 fig newton cookies	1 tbsp. chopped nuts
½ cup Port or Muscatel	

Crumble fig newtons, mix with nuts, and moisten with wine. Heap into dessert glasses. Chill for about 30 minutes, and serve, topped with custard sauce.

WINE PLUM PUDDING (*12 to 16 servings*)

1 cup seedless raisins	2 cups fine bread crumbs
½ cup diced candied orange and lemon peels	¾ cup sugar
	½ cup flour
½ cup diced citron	½ tsp. salt
½ cup sliced candied cherries	½ tsp. cloves
	1 tsp. cinnamon
¾ cup Sherry	1 tsp. nutmeg
1 cup chopped kidney suet	½ cup chopped walnuts
	6 eggs, well beaten

Combine fruits. Add wine and let stand several hours, or overnight. Combine other ingredients in order given.

Add fruit in wine and mix well. Pour into one large ring (1½ or 2 quarts) mold or bowl; cover tightly. Set mold on rack in kettle. Pour boiling water around it, letting water come up well on sides of mold. Cover kettle, and boil vigorously for 3½ hours. Add more hot water as needed. Serve at once, if desired, or cool and store in cold place until needed, then resteam about 1 hour, or until thoroughly heated. Serve hot with Creamy Wine Sauce.

Creamy Wine Sauce (Yield: 1½ cups)

- ¾ cup honey or light corn syrup
- ½ cup top milk
- 2 tbsps. soft margarine
- 1 tbsp. flour
- 1 egg yolk, beaten
- ¼ cup Sherry

Heat honey or light corn syrup and milk. Blend margarine and flour. Add. Cook, stirring, until smooth. Stir in beaten egg yolk, and cook, stirring, 1 minute longer. Add wine, and serve hot over puddings.

WINE FRUIT CAKE (*Makes 6 lbs.*)

- 1 lb. white raisins
- ½ lb. citron
- ¾ lb. candied cherries
- 1 lb. candied pineapple
- ¼ lb. mixed orange and lemon peel
- 1 lb. nut meats
- 3 cups sifted flour
- 2 tsps. baking powder
- ½ tsp. salt
- 1 cup shortening
- 1 cup sugar
- 5 eggs
- ⅓ cup Port, Muscatel or Tokay
- 1 tsp. vanilla extract
- ½ tsp. almond extract

Chop fruits and nuts and mix thoroughly with 1 cup flour. Sift remaining 2 cups flour with baking powder and salt. Cream shortening, gradually add sugar, and cream well. Add the eggs, one at a time, and beat vigorously after each addition. Add sifted dry ingredients to mixture alternately with wine and extracts. Fold in floured fruits and nuts. Pour into pans which have been greased and lined with wax paper. Bake in a pan of water in a slow oven (300 degrees F.) for 2 to 2½ hours, or steam in a steamer for 1 hour and bake 1½ hours. Remove from pan. Peel off the paper and cool on cake rack.

To store fruit cake: Wrap in cloth moistened with wine and in wax paper. Store in pans in which cakes were baked. Place pans in stone crock or other covered container. Sprinkle small amount of wine over cloth-wrapping occasionally to keep cloth slightly moist with wine. Store 1 to 2 weeks before cutting.

WINE FRUIT BARS (*Yield: 40 squares*)

- 2 cups flour
- ½ tsp. baking soda
- ½ tsp. salt
- ½ tsp. nutmeg
- 1 cup raisins, chopped prunes, currants, or any dried chopped fruit
- ½ cup butter or margarine
- ⅔ cup brown sugar, firmly packed
- 1 egg
- ¼ cup Port or Muscatel

Mix and sift dry ingredients. Mix fruit with dry ingredients. Cream the butter or margarine, add the sugar, and cream well. Beat the egg into the butter-sugar mixture. Add dry ingredients to mixture alternately with the wine. Pour onto an oiled cookie sheet. Spread evenly, and bake in a moderately hot oven (375 degrees F.) for about 12 minutes. Cut into bars while still warm. Cool, and ice with Wine Frosting.

Wine Frosting

1 tbsp. butter or margarine
1½ cups confectioner's sugar
½ tsp. nutmeg
Port or Muscatel to moisten to spreading consistency

Blend butter or margarine into sugar. Add nutmeg and enough wine to bring mixture to smooth spreading consistency.

CHERRY PORT SAUCE

1 cup cherry conserve or currant jelly
3 tbsps. lemon juice
3 tbsps. butter
1 tbsp. cornstarch
¼ tsp. cinnamon
1 cup Port

Add lemon juice to cherry conserve or currant jelly. Melt butter. Add cornstarch, and blend to smooth paste. Add cherry or currant mixture, cinnamon, and Port. Cook very slowly, stirring constantly, until slightly thickened. Serve with custards or plain puddings.

TOKAY CREAM SAUCE

¼ cup butter or margarine
1 cup confectioner's sugar
2 eggs, beaten
1 cup Tokay, Muscatel, or Port
Grated rind of 1 lemon

Cream butter. Add sugar, and beat until light. Add beaten eggs gradually, beating with a rotary beater after each addition. Place over boiling water, and add wine and grated lemon rind. Whip until light and fluffy. Serve with puddings.

SHERRIED CUSTARD SAUCE (*Serves 6*)

2 cups milk
3 eggs or 6 yolks
¼ cup Sherry
¼ cup sugar
⅛ tsp. salt

Heat milk in double boiler. Beat eggs or yolks slightly with sugar and salt. Add the hot milk a little at a time, stirring constantly, then return all to double boiler and cook over hot (not boiling) water, still stirring constantly, until the mixture will coat a metal spoon. Remove at once from hot water, strain, cool, and stir in Sherry. Serve chilled, poured over desserts such as wine jelly.

TAWNY WINE SAUCE

¼ cup butter
2 cups brown sugar
2 egg yolks
1 cup cream
½ cup Port or Tokay

Cream butter with sugar. Add egg yolks. Stir in the cream gradually. Heat over boiling water until thickened. Remove from over hot water. Add wine. Serve with puddings.

LEMON WINE SAUCE (*Serves 8*)

1 cup sugar
3 tbsps. cornstarch
½ tsp. salt
1½ cups boiling water
2 egg yolks, slightly beaten
6 tbsps. lemon juice
2 tsps. grated lemon rind
½ cup Muscatel or Port
2 tbsps. butter or margarine

Combine sugar, cornstarch, and salt. Add hot water gradually, and cook mixture in double boiler, stirring occasionally, until thickened and clear. Pour small amount of hot water over beaten egg yolks. Stir into sauce. Add lemon juice, lemon rind, and wine. Cook 1 minute, stirring constantly. Add the butter before removing from heat. Cool, and serve over squares of plain cake.

WINE HARD SAUCE

⅓ cup butter
1 egg yolk
3 tbsps. Sherry
2 cups confectioner's sugar

Cream the butter thoroughly. Add the egg yolk, and continue creaming mixture. Blend in the sugar, adding enough wine to make a hard sauce of the right consistency.

CHAPTER 12

COCKTAILS, COOLERS, COBBLERS, AND WINE PUNCHES

Then a smile, and a glass, and a toast, and
a cheer,
For all the good wine, and we've some of it
here.

OLIVER WENDELL HOLMES

Many of these recipes date back for hundreds of years, for wine has long been the time-honored beverage of hospitality. Here are the Port Negus, immortalized in Charles Dickens's *Christmas Carol;* the Wassail Bowle which was for centuries the traditional toast to the New Year; Eggnog that's as much a part of our Christmas holidays as mistletoe and Santa Claus, and May Wine to celebrate the arrival of spring. Here are Champagne bowls for weddings, anniversaries, and special occasions, and a variety of delicious wine-and-fruit punches for informal parties. Included are short drinks and long drinks, wine cups for year-'round service, and hot wine drinks that are cheerful and warming when the wintry winds blow.

The coolers and cobblers, usually served in tall tumblers or highball glasses, provide ideal refreshment for bridge and card parties and impromptu get-togethers. The wine cocktails may be offered before dinner or for evening refreshment.

Good companions with any of these wine beverages

are cheese and crackers, nuts, cookies, small cakes, or thin-cut sandwiches.

ALL AMERICAN COCKTAIL (*2 servings*)

4 oz. Burgundy or Claret
1 tbsp. sugar
1 oz. lemon juice

Combine ingredients, and shake with ice cubes. Strain into cocktail glasses.

BAMBOO COCKTAIL

1½ oz. Sherry
1½ oz. Sweet Vermouth
Dash of bitters

Combine Sherry, Sweet Vermouth, and bitters in a cocktail glass. Stir (but don't shake) in cracked ice. Strain, and serve.

CHAMPAGNE COCKTAIL

Place ½ tsp. sugar in a wide-brimmed glass. Add a dash of bitters and well-chilled Champagne to fill. Stir very little. A twist of lemon peel may be added.

CLARET FLIP

1½ tbsps. fine sugar
1 egg
¾ cup Claret or Burgundy

Combine sugar, egg, and wine. Add ice cubes, and shake thoroughly. Strain into tall glass, and top with nutmeg.

CLUB COCKTAIL

1½ oz. Port
1½ oz. Sherry
Dash of orange bitters

Combine ingredients in a large cocktail or old-fashioned glass with 2 or 3 ice cubes. Stir, and serve.

PORT COCKTAIL

1½ oz. Port
1½ oz. Dry Vermouth
Dash orange bitters

Combine Port, Dry Vermouth, and orange bitters in a cocktail glass. Stir in cracked ice. Strain, but do not shake. Serve.

SHERRY FLIP

1 egg
3 oz. Sherry
1 tsp. fine granulated sugar

Combine egg, sugar, and Sherry, and shake with ice cubes. Strain, and pour.

SHERRY OLD-FASHIONED

½ tsp. sugar
3 oz. Sherry
Dash of bitters
Maraschino cherry
Twist of lemon peel
Half slice orange

To the sugar add bitters, ice cubes, lemon peel, maraschino cherry, and a slice of orange. Pour in Sherry, stir well, and serve. Be sure to twist the lemon peel inside the glass so the oil will flavor the drink.

WHITE WINE COCKTAIL

3 oz. Sauterne or Rhine Wine
Bitters
Twist of lemon peel

Add a dash of bitters to the chilled wine in a cocktail glass. Add twist of lemon peel, and serve.

CLARET WINE COOLER

½ glass Claret
Ice cubes
Sparkling water

Pour half a tall glass of Claret over 3 or 4 ice cubes. Add sparkling water to fill, stir slightly, and serve. If desired, an orange or lemon slice may be used to decorate. For flavor variety this same cooler may also be made with Burgundy, Sauterne, or Rhine Wine.

GINGEREE

1 tsp. sugar
2 tsps. lemon juice
3 oz. Port or Muscatel
1 egg
Ginger ale

Dissolve sugar in lemon juice and add wine and egg. Shake vigorously with ice cubes. Strain into tall glass, filling glass ¾ full. Add ice-cold ginger ale to fill. Stir, and serve.

SAUTERNE FIZZ

3 oz. Sauterne
Juice of ½ lemon
Juice of ½ orange
1 tbsp. Grenadine

Combine in a tall tumbler, add ice cubes, and fill with sparkling water.

SHERRY COBBLER

1 tsp. sugar	3 oz. Sherry
1 tbsp. lemon juice	Cracked ice

Dissolve sugar in Sherry in a tall glass. Add lemon juice. Fill glass with cracked ice. Stir well and serve with straws.

WHITE GRAPE COBBLER

1½ tsps. sugar	White seedless grapes
4 oz. Sauterne or Rhine Wine	

Dissolve sugar in the wine in a tall glass. Fill glass with cracked ice, and stir well. Ornament with white seedless grapes, and serve with straws. A slice of orange or strawberries may be added, if desired.

PORT WINE COBBLER

½ tsp. sugar	2 tsps. lemon juice
3 oz. Port or Muscatel	

Moisten sugar with lemon juice in bottom of tall glass. Add wine. Fill glass with cracked ice, and stir. Add a slice of orange, and serve with straws.

PINEAPPLE CLARET PUNCH (*Serves 6 to 8*)

3 cups Claret	¼ cup lemon juice
2 cups unsweetened pineapple juice	1 cup sparkling water

Chill Claret, pineapple juice, and sparkling water. Combine in a punch bowl or large water pitcher. Add lemon juice and sugar to taste. Garnish with lemon slices.

ICED SHERRY EGGNOG (*2 servings*)

1 egg
½ cup milk or cream
4 ice cubes
½ cup Sherry
1 tsp. sugar

Add milk or cream to the egg. Add the Sherry, sugar, and ice cubes. Shake well, then remove ice and pour. Fleck with nutmeg.

SAUTERNE FRUIT PUNCH (*Serves 10 to 12*)

2 bottles Sauterne
2 cups sliced peaches
½ cup sugar
3 tbsps. lemon juice
½ cup water
Lemon rind

Dissolve sugar in water. Add lemon juice and few strips lemon rind. Pour over a block of ice in a chilled punch bowl and add Sauterne. Add fruit just before serving. Sliced oranges, strawberries, or other fruit may be used and may be slightly sugared. Serve in punch cups or small glasses.

CLARET WINE LEMONADE

1½ tbsps. lemon juice
4 ounces Claret
1 tbsp. sugar

Dissolve sugar in lemon juice. Add Claret, and shake with ice cubes until cold. Pour over ice cubes in tall glass. Add chilled sparkling water or plain ice water to fill. Stir, and serve decorated with lemon slices. This wine lemonade may also be made with Burgundy, Rhine Wine, or Sauterne.

CHAMPAGNE CLARET PUNCH (*Serves 25 to 30*)

2 bottles Champagne
2 bottles Claret
2 bottles sparkling water
Half lemon rind
Juice of 1 lemon
½ cup maraschino syrup
4 tbsps. sugar

Chill the Champagne, Claret, and sparkling water. Shred the lemon rind into punch bowl, and add sugar. Add lemon juice and maraschino syrup. Stir well. Place a large square block of ice in punch bowl, and add the well-chilled sparkling water, Claret, and Champagne. Stir just enough to mix well. Ornament with fruit in season, and serve.

MAY WINE (*Serves 12 to 15*)

2 bottles Sauterne
¼ cup sugar
1 cup orange juice
1 cup strawberries, sliced
2 oranges, sliced

Chill wine. Dissolve sugar in orange juice in chilled punch bowl. Add Sauterne, sliced strawberries, and orange slices. Float a few flowers on surface of punch just before serving.

CHAMPAGNE WEDDING PUNCH (*Serves 30*)

2 bottles Champagne
1 bottle Sauterne
4 cups canned pineapple, cubed
1½ quarts ice water
1 quart strawberries, fresh or frozen
3 cups sugar
2 cups lemon juice

Chill Champagne and Sauterne thoroughly. Dissolve sugar in lemon juice. Combine in a punch bowl with pineapple. Add a square block of ice. Add chilled Sauterne and ice water. Add strawberries and chilled Champagne just before serving.

PINK PARTY PUNCH (*Serves 12*)

- 2 bottles Burgundy or Claret
- Juice and peel of 2 lemons
- 1 cup sugar
- 1 bottle sparkling water

Combine ingredients and stir well in punch bowl with cubes of ice. Chill thoroughly. Remove lemon peel, and serve. Sliced oranges may be added.

CLARET CHERRY BOWL (*Serves 12*)

- 4 cups Claret or Burgundy
- 2 cups pitted red cherries
- 1 cup water
- ½ cup sugar
- 1 stick cinnamon
- 2 cups sparkling water

Make a syrup with the sugar and water. Bring to boiling point. Add cherries and stick cinnamon, and cook slowly for 10 minutes. Cool, remove cinnamon, and chill. Add chilled wine to the cherry juice and the cherries. Add the sparkling water immediately before serving.

CALIFORNIA PUNCH

- 1 part orange juice
- 2 parts Claret or Burgundy

Combine the orange juice (or grapefruit juice) and wine. Add ice cubes and serve. If desired, a few sprigs of fresh mint and sugar to taste may be added.

HOT WINE LEMONADE

1 tbsp. sugar
6 tbsps. water
1½ tbsps. lemon juice
3 ounces Port

Dissolve sugar in lemon juice in saucepan. Add water and Port. Heat, but do not boil, and serve in glass.

SAUTERNE TODDY

½ glass Sauterne
Boiling water
Sugar

Heat Sauterne. Pour into glass, and fill with boiling water. Add sugar to taste. Garnish with twist of lemon peel.

PORT NEGUS (*8 servings*)

1 bottle Port
1 lemon
2 tbsps. sugar
1 cup boiling water

Pare off yellow rind of lemon. Place rind and juice of lemon in top of double boiler. Add sugar and Port, and heat to boiling. Stir in 1 cup boiling water; strain into mugs or glasses. If glasses are used, put a spoon in each while pouring. Fleck with nutmeg, and serve.

HOT MULLED WINE
(*Hot Spiced Wine—Serves 10 to 15*)

1 cup sugar
3 cups boiling water
Half lemon rind
18 whole cloves
6 inches stick cinnamon
2 bottles Claret or Burgundy

Dissolve sugar in boiling water. Add lemon rind, cloves, and cinnamon. Boil together for 15 minutes. Strain into double boiler and add wine. Heat piping hot, but do not boil. Serve flecked with nutmeg.

HOT MULLED WINE
(*Hot Spiced Wine—1 serving*)

5 oz. Claret or Burgundy
1 tbsp. sugar
2 slices lemon
Cinnamon and nutmeg

To the wine add the sugar, lemon slices, and a dash each of cinnamon and nutmeg. Heat to boiling, but do not boil. Serve hot, in a toddy or old-fashioned glass.

HOT SHERRY EGGNOG (*Serves 12*)

1 qt. milk
⅓ cup sugar
2 cups Sherry
4 egg yolks
¼ tsp. each nutmeg, cinnamon, and vanilla

Scald milk in double boiler. Beat egg yolks slightly with sugar and spices. Stir a little of the hot milk into egg mixture, then return all to double boiler and cook, stirring, for 3 or 4 minutes. Stir in Sherry slowly. Heat thoroughly, and serve.

WASSAIL BOWL (*Serves 8 to 10*)

6 baked apples
½ tsp. nutmeg
½ tsp. cinnamon
3 cloves
4 eggs, beaten separately
½ cup sugar
1 tbsp. grated lemon rind
2 bottles Sherry or Muscatel

Core the apples and peel down about 1 inch from stem end. Fill core cavities with sugar, and bake in a moderate oven until tender. Add nutmeg, cinnamon, cloves, sugar, and lemon rind to the wine, and heat in a double boiler. Fold the beaten egg yolks into the stiffly beaten whites. Add the hot wine liquid gradually; beat vigorously to froth the mixture.

Place the baked apples in the bottom of the Wassail Bowle and pour the hot liquid over them. Serve in warm mugs.

ARCHBISHOP (*Serves 4 to 6*)

Juice of 2 oranges
Pared rind of ½ orange
2 doz. whole cloves
1 bottle Burgundy or Claret
½ cup sugar

Combine orange juice, orange rind, and cloves, and heat in double boiler for 15 minutes. Strain. Put back in double boiler, and add wine. Stir in sugar, and heat thoroughly. Bishop is made the same way, using Port and lemons in place of the Claret or Burgundy and oranges, and less sugar.

HOT CLARET CHEERIO (*9 servings*)

1½ cups apple juice or prune juice
3 tbsps. sugar or honey
3 inches stick cinnamon
12 whole cloves
3 slices lemon
1 bottle Claret or Burgundy

Boil the apple juice (or prune juice), sugar or honey, cinnamon, and cloves for 5 minutes. Strain, add the wine, and heat, but do not boil. Serve hot.

Index

www.ingramcontent.com/pod-product-compliance
Lightning Source LLC
Chambersburg PA
CBHW070842100426
42813CB00003B/716
* 9 7 8 0 8 9 4 9 6 1 2 0 5 *